Pitching
HOLLYWOOD

How to Sell Your
TV and Movie Ideas

Pitching
HOLLYWOOD

How to Sell Your
TV and Movie Ideas

Jonathan Koch and Robert Kosberg
with Tanya Meurer Norman

Quill Driver Books

Word Dancer Press

Sanger, California

*Printed in the United States of America
Published by Quill Driver Books/Word Dancer Press, Inc.
1831 Industrial Way #101
Sanger, California 93657
559-876-2170 • 1-800-497-4909 • FAX 559-876-2180
QuillDriverBooks.com
Info@QuillDriverBooks.com*

Quill Driver Books' titles may be purchased in
quantity at special discounts for educational, fund-raising,
business, or promotional use. Please contact Special
Markets, Quill Driver Books/Word Dancer Press, Inc. at the
above address or at 1-800-497-4909.

Quill Driver Books/Word Dancer Press, Inc. project cadre:
Susan Klassen, John David Marion, Cheree McCloud,
Stephen Blake Mettee, Brigitte Phillips

First Printing

To order another copy of this book, please call
1-800-497-4909

Library of Congress Cataloging-in-Publication Data

Koch, Jonathan.
    Pitching Hollywood : how to sell your TV and movie ideas / by Jonathan
Koch and Robert Kosberg with Tanya Meurer Norman.
       p. cm.
    Includes bibliographical references.
    ISBN 1-884956-31-9
      1. Television authorship--Marketing. 2. Motion picture authorship--Market-
ing. I. Kosberg, Robert. II. Norman, Tanya Meurer. III. Title.

PN1992.7.K63 2004
808.2'3--dc22

2004004495

Dedicated to

Tom and Sharon

Heartfelt thanks to

Richard Allen

Mitch Baranowski

Robert Bennett

The Cameron Family

Joshua Clark

Elske Cordero

Deep Ellum Film Festival

Melissa Havard

Jeff Hays

Mike Heard

Stephanie Hunt

Sally Kemp

Mike Lankford

Alan Larson

Leslie MacCambridge

Greg Mansur

Steve Mettee

N.A.T.P.E.

Steve Nemeth (The Epicenter)

Amanda Norman

Nick Norman

Stephanie Palmer

Mildred A. Peveto

Karen Troy Powers

Bobby Pura

Farris Rookstool III

Sheila Rosenbaum

Greg Strangis

T.C.U.

U.S.C.

Richard Underhill

and... Sean Welch

Contents

Foreword

One-liner, high-concept pitches are the most effective pitches, and Robert Kosberg, "King of the Pitch," is famous in the industry for his arsenal of high-concept ideas. He, Jonathan Koch, and other pitchmen have been able to create careers in the selling of ideas to Hollywood for money, producer credit, co-story credit, created by credit, etc. While I always encourage those who pitch mere ideas to go sit down and write a script or pay someone else to do so, these guys prove that scripts aren't always necessary. Regardless of your project's form (idea, treatment, script, or even completed film), you'll need to know how to pitch it effectively.

As head of Rhino Films and an independent producer, part of my job is to acquire new entertainment properties. I often take three to five pitches a day. New material constantly comes through my office, and I welcome it, since fresh ideas provide for a steady flow of projects and deals. I love to hear a great idea pitched well.

It has been said that the definition of a producer is anyone who knows a writer. I'll take that a step further: Anyone with a great piece of material can position himself or herself to become a producer! Just pitch it!

And, material is everywhere. It's in the paper, on the news, a story told by a friend. It may be the plot in your favorite book or an original idea, designed by your imagination. While good ideas are easily found, great ideas are not. Great ideas are rare, and it's important to learn how to recognize them. You've got to take into account the many components of salability and learn the market.

Do your homework and target the appropriate buyers, as the right idea in the wrong office is a waste of everyone's time. Once you've fleshed out that great idea and set up meetings, you must be able to pitch it perfectly. This is not optional. A botched pitch can kill even the most brilliant idea. I even will go so far as to say this: A great pitch for a mediocre project can be as effective as mediocre pitch for a dynamite project. No matter how amazing your idea may be, before pitching it, you must master the skill.

Understand that pitching is an elusive art, one that is filled with contradictions. Your potential buyer should find you passionate and wildly enthusiastic about the project, yet credible, well-grounded, and realistic.

Pitches must be short, but not so short as to leave the scene unset. They must contain all of the pertinent details—but not so many as to lose a buyer's attention. Wordy pitches can be boring and counter-productive. Give the buyer credit. We have imaginations and can fill in the blanks. Convey the tone and the spirit of your idea without the words, words, words. But be aware: Leaving out key info will create confusion, and you will be interrupted with questions. As a pitcher, you must appear personable and strong, but you should never initiate deadly, chatty small-talk. Our time together should be productive, but also as brief as possible. The acquiring and fine-tuning of these precise skills is essential.

Educate yourself. Know what you are up against. The majority of the producers and execs to whom you'll be pitching think they are better at recognizing a great idea than you are and they are certain they know more than you. On top of that, they have short attention spans and limited time. Study the art of the pitch, practice it, and learn it. Your odds for success in this business (and any other) will go up considerably.

—Stephen Nemeth, CEO, Rhino Films

Chapter 1

Who We Are

We are known as Hollywood "pitchmen." Our job is to create and find interesting TV shows and movie ideas and then produce them. We make appointments with studios and production companies, and we sell ideas to them. We do this in L.A., full-time, and make a very nice income and lead enjoyable lives.

To us, it's the best job on earth.

Bob:

I'm a producer. By selling your ideas and carefully negotiating your deal, you can become a producer too. It's not hard.

When I went to UCLA, there was a screenwriting division, a filmmaking division, and an editing division. I couldn't hold a camera. I couldn't edit. By default, I picked screenwriting, which was great. The trouble came after graduation, when I couldn't get a job, and I had no way to make a living.

So I wrote a script. You know, after you're through writing it, you put in a drawer and then tell people you're a writer. In turn they ask, "And how do you make a living?"

I bounced from job to job. I worked in public relations. I was a script reader for a prestigious Hollywood talent agency. I was a celebrity assistant. Anything to learn about the business and pay bills.

I eventually worked in Malibu for an A-list actress who was going through emotional upheaval. My first day with her, I heard a shriek coming from the upstairs bedroom. She was practicing her primal scream therapy, and she told me that she had neither the time nor the presence of mind to meet with me. My interview ended up being with her 7-year-old daughter. I took this daughter to lunch and was promptly arrested on the Pacific Coast Highway, accused of kidnapping.

And that's how you get jobs in Hollywood.

After reading scripts for the actress, I went to New York and read for a producer, and here's what happened: I learned how easy it is to be a producer. My New York producer-boss was off in Europe making a movie. One day, I was sitting behind the absent boss' desk, and I saw an article in the *New York Times* about a boy who graduated college and went back to high school. For a year he pretended to be a senior. He wanted to meet girls; he wanted to be on the gymnastics team; he wanted to make good grades and do all the things that he hadn't done the first time around. It was the old going-back-in-time plot, but this kid did it without time travel. This kid actually went back and pretended to be a high school student. So I picked up the phone, and I tracked him down.

I found him in Wichita, Kansas. Now remember: My boss was away, and I was behind his desk. I told the kid, "I'm a producer, and I want to buy the rights to your story. I will to pay you $500." He agreed.

Later, when the contract had been drawn up, I asked him which other producers had called him. He said, "You were the only one."

That's my point. There are incredible stories every day in the newspaper, which can become fabulous films. You should never assume that everybody in Hollywood is smarter than you or faster than you or has more money than you. This erroneous assumption shouldn't stop you from acquiring material. I bought the rights to that story, and I pitched it around New York and L.A. I sold it. It never got made into a movie, but it was my first producing deal. It started my career, first as a writer and later as a producer. Within a year I had my first writing/producing deal at Disney Studios. I look back now and realize that it all started by making a photocopy of an article. So, my first suggestion is: Start reading and photocopying.

The *L.A. Times* ran a story about the "Woo-Woo Kid": A fourteen-year-old boy who had been touted as America's greatest lover in the 1940s. Fourteen-years-old and the world's greatest lover?! I looked it up in the

UCLA archives, and there he was. My parents were from the same generation, and they remembered him. Sure enough, he was a real, live person with a legendary reputation as a teenage ladies' man.

I tracked him down and found him living in Las Vegas. He was 60-years old at the time and driving a tour bus, but at 14-years-old, back in the forties he was the famous Woo-Woo Kid. I bought the rights and pitched the story. My writing partner David Simon and I were hired to write the first draft. Ultimately it was produced as *In the Mood*. It was *Field of Dreams* writer/director Phil Robinson's first project and starred Patrick Dempsey.

I went on to secure more producer credits, including such films as *Commando*, starring Arnold Schwarzenegger, and more recently, *Twelve Monkeys* with Brad Pitt and Bruce Willis. I've produced a spate of TV shows and movies. All of these projects began with that one photocopied newspaper article, the rights to which I bought for $500.

PHOTOCOPYING

Now I am based at Nash Entertainment and I am still photocopying. I spend my days pitching stories on the phone and in studio production development offices. I have working relationships with key creative executives at all of the major studios in Hollywood. I also work with dozens of independent production companies. I pitch to all of them and continue to sell them all sorts of stories and ideas. To date, I have approximately 30 feature projects sold, and they are in active development at various studios.

It comes down to material. If you can find the material (whether it's an idea that you dream up tonight, an idea your mother tells you on the telephone, or an idea from an article in the newspaper), if you can effectively pitch that material to Hollywood, you are a pitchman. When you make a sale, you can become a writer or producer, too.

Jonathan:

My journey has been a wild one. Thirty-one hours after graduating from Shippensburg University in Pennsylvania, I arrived in Los Angeles with a duffel bag full of clothes, $300, and a half eaten Hostess pudding pie. I knew nearly nobody and even less about what I wanted to do.

Two weeks later: My car had been stolen, I'd been fired from my job as a waiter, and had been booed off stage at a local comedy club. It was a bit overwhelming, but I knew that easier times lay ahead.

I credit my first boss, Rich Moran, with much of my early success. Rich was one of the most successful commercial real estate agents in town when I started working as his assistant. He was decidedly difficult to work for, but he hammered home the critical value of tenacity, cold calling, and the idea that nobody in business is doing you a favor. It is all about the deal, and that's it. I have never forgotten his "if you want a friend, buy a dog" approach to business. Of course, I have great relationships and friendships in (and out) of the showbiz, but I learned from his basic business elements: a strong work ethic, originality, and a lot of luck.

At twenty-three years old, I left real estate at the urging of my then business partner and extraordinary friend, Bill Schumer. One day, he sat me down and asked me what my passions were. He must have sensed my discomfort with such an odd question, and he carefully clarified that he was talking about my business life. Whew! He knew that my heart wasn't really in real estate and that entertainment was my true passion. We had a lucrative partnership and both felt we were destined for amazing success, but Bill, without my asking, picked up the phone and called some entertainment friends to set up interviews for me. He went on to enjoy phenomenal success in real estate, but he gave me the opportunity to compete in the field of my true passion. We are still good friends, and he continues to inspire me.

Before tackling the rigors of pitching and selling ideas and projects, I was the worst nonworking actor in this town. To this day, when casting directors suffer through particularly bad auditions, they call each other and say, "I just saw a Jonathan." The truth hurts sometimes, but I'm over it now.

The list goes on and on. I worked as an agent, manager, pseudo-lawyer, and in various entertainment related fields.

Now, I am an entertainment entrepreneur. I will consider and often attack any size or type of deal within the entertainment field. Aside from producing, I've had an Internet business, a NFL license for women's apparel and lingerie, a concert venue in Anaheim, and other commercial ventures. I love the hunt. It's down and dirty, a high stakes poker game that's played out in the world's most scrutinized and publicized pit.

As an independent producer, deal making is how I spend my day. I love it. I love making money with my brain. I love the people. I love succeeding and failing on my own terms. When things go well, I have many people to thank. When things go wrong, I can usually look to myself for the reasons, learn from them, and move forward.

It is a unique business, a business which supports fearless, creative warriors who are willing to risk rejection, endure sporadic paydays, and subject themselves to personal ridicule.

I love it.

Bob and I met when he was working for Merv Griffin Entertainment and I was an agent. He was pitching an idea to my client, Jonathan Taylor Thomas, at the "Home Improvement" set. One day, I told Bob about a game show concept, which we ended up taking to Mr. Griffin. Two months later I found myself working for Griffin's company. Bob and I became a team and began our pitching days there, selling movies to television.

I am currently based at Asylum Entertainment at Fox in Los Angeles. I spend my days collecting/creating, pitching, and selling ideas to Hollywood. I watch TV. I read. I listen to people. Material is everywhere.

Chapter 2

Who You Are
(and Why You Are Reading This Book)

We are writing this book for everyone, since it's possible for anyone to have an idea that could be made into a TV show or film. Maybe you are reading this book because you are a film student, and this book is on your required reading list. Maybe you work in the entertainment industry and want some tips on handling pitch meetings.

Or, maybe you are a stockbroker in New York, or you day-trade as a day job or you are a new mom, a high school student, a retired Army officer, the sheriff in a small Midwestern town or you teach Sunday school, tend bar, clean houses, build race cars.

Whatever it is that you do, if you've picked up this book and plan to read it, you most likely are an idea person.

IDEA PEOPLE

Idea people are creative types, people who can watch world events and see them for their most fundamental elements. As an idea person, you can distance yourself from the event and view the individuals involved more like characters than actual people. You possess the ability to strip away the emotions of a disaster and process the news story as a plotline.

While this might sound cold and mean on paper, it's really not. Some of the best ideas in Hollywood are born this way.

For instance, if a ship sinks in a faraway sea, those who have no personal connection to the people who died in the tragedy can, with minimal effort, dismiss it. Being interested in disasters that only directly effect us is more common than not. What's not common is the detached processing of an event with the goal of generating a storyline.

Idea people look for sad, interesting, funny, ironic, pitiful, uplifting, and tragic storylines. These storylines might serve as a backdrop for characters completely unrelated to the actual event. That sinking ship might be moved to the Texas Gulf Coast and be a mere subplot for a bigger story. Maybe the sinking ship is the entire story. Maybe the story begins with an escape from the ship. The ship might become part of a reality game show. Idea people will mentally file that sinking ship and save it for later use.

No friend, no family member is safe from the idea person. Even acquaintances and strangers are fair game. They can be used as characters or character templates in multiple storylines. Conversations can become dialogue. This, too, is neither cold nor mean. It's efficient and it can be quite profitable.

The eyes and ears (and all of the other senses) of the idea person are constantly gathering information to be used later. This input, when assembled carefully, can become great TV or film ideas. Those ideas are entertainment properties, and they can be sold.

Selling Your Ideas as Property

You don't have to live in Los Angeles to sell your ideas to Hollywood. If you want to make films or run a production company, it might be a good idea to live in L.A., since it is the entertainment capital of the world. If you are currently a film student, you are probably planning on this. Marinating in the industry, working your way up through the ranks, and making friends and contacts in the business will be important for your career. For you, honing your pitching skills is vital.

If you'd like to continue your job as a police officer in Portland but have some ideas that you'd like to try and sell, stay put. Stay in Portland. You are gathering fantastic material in your job as a cop. Take advantage of that. Could you imagine if every film idea came from Southern California?

The industry needs the whole world of experiences that are out there, folks. The majority of TV audiences and filmgoers live in what has been termed: the Fly-over States. Middle America is what drives the industry. If you live in Tennessee, you have access to people and places that studio executives never see. Think about this. Even if they could visit your region, they would view those people and places with different eyes, missing the important regional nuisances.

Hollywood needs the Everyman. If you are an Everyman who is also an idea person, you could make a good deal of money and have a whole lot of fun. But first, you must refine your ideas and perfect your pitch.

Read on.

Chapter 3

How We Created Our Positions

Bob:

I don't mean to diminish the value of all producers, everywhere, but those of you reading this book have the same ability to read newspapers and make photocopies that I do. It's not that difficult. For the last fifteen years I've done that same thing: read newspapers and photocopy stories. I also listen to the news, watching for stories and events that are intriguing. I formulate those real life happenings into pitchable ideas.

But the real key lies in the pitching. If you can't effectively pitch your idea to a producer or development executive, you can't sell it. I'm good at pitching. Over time, the execs in town have gotten to know me, so it's become increasingly easy for me to get meetings with them.

Jonathan:

You've got to experience life. You've got to take chances. I have people ask me how I got this "job" all of the time. The fact is that Bob and I both got into the industry in weird ways: I met Kirk Cameron ("Growing Pains") on the one and only occasion I ever bowled in my life. He later introduced me to his mother and my future business partner, Barbara Cameron. And Bob got his start by being arrested for kidnapping a 7-year-old.

Bob:

No, I slept my way to top. Or at least the middle.

Jonathan:

Remember the list of all of those jobs I had before becoming a pitchman? I learned about being in front of the camera in my acting classes. I learned about business in real estate. I learned about people by being a waiter. By the time I partnered with Barbara Cameron's Agency, I was ready to tackle anything. Just living my life, watching the people and events going on around me, prepared me for pitching.

My biggest asset is that I am fearless, 100% fearless. I call anybody; I say anything. I do anything that will, within the context of my business plan, move me forward. Understand that I do not lie; if you have a great concept, lying can only harm you. I get into the roots of people. I need them to hear me. I can't let them tell me no. I can't let their assistants tell me no, even though it's their job to do exactly that.

Here is the toughest hurtle: capturing your talent or rising above your lack of it. Now, this is some sound advice. If you aren't a gifted speaker, all is not lost. You will just have to work a little harder.

Talent isn't the issue. You have to get yourself to the point where you are not afraid to get out there and make the phone calls to people who can make decisions. If they say no to you, make it more difficult for them to say no. Be persistent and make sure that your idea gets heard.

Bob:

You have to go into the movie business knowing it's a Wild, Wild West mentality. The successful people in L.A. or New York are the people who are willing to ride into that world, bounce around with it, find where they are the happiest, and can make a living. I found that in pitching and writing.

I felt uncomfortable when I first started producing. I didn't know anything about producing so I thought: Well, I'll be a coproducer. I know a lot about "co-ing." I teamed up with a screenwriter. We'd been friends in New York, and I was always amazed at his confidence level. He had no idea what the L.A. film world was about. He just thought he would come out here, team up with me, and go sell ideas. I thought he was crazy, but I had sold a project and gotten an agent. The agent set up a few meetings for us, so it was definitely worth a try.

We walked into one of these meetings and simply pitched a page of ideas. The shocked executives said, "You guys are in here, pitching us ideas, telling us you want to be screenwriters, and you don't even have a writing sample between the two of you. What are you doing in here?" It seemed we were challenging the established rules.

I said, "Well, is it okay that we are here? We have ideas. We drove out to meet with you. We are here. Let us at least give you these ideas we have."

And sure enough, some of those ideas were so good that we changed the rules. And that goes to prove: There are no rules.

Jonathan:
We created our positions by breaking nonexistent rules.

Chapter 4

What Is "High Concept"?

In the next chapter we will cover the anatomy of a good idea. It's basic elements are surprisingly definable. But before we go a step further, let's get this term defined and out of the way.

For the most part, pitches are under five minutes. Anything longer than five minutes will bore most people. The story must have a beginning, middle, and end—often called a "three-act structure." It must be fresh and commercial. It must be told with great zeal. The best, most salable pitches have a well-defined "high concept."

High concept is the meat of the story or show summed up in one or two sentences. High concepts can be outrageous, funny, controversial, poignant, or any of a number of things, but they must grab the listener's attention and create an immediate visual image in his mind:

> A boy meets a girl, and she turns out to be a mermaid: *Splash*.
> A man can't get a job as an actor, so he puts on a dress: *Tootsie*.
> Boy makes a wish to be big, and you have a child in an adult's body: *Big*.
> MTV cops: "Miami Vice."

If you can describe a high concept idea to a buyer in one sentence, the buyer knows he can explain it to investors, potential cast and crew members, and viewers in one sentence. That same sentence can be slapped on a movie poster or billboard, serving as a logline.

Usually a high concept will have a gimmick or a twist. Many fantasy films are high concept. Babies talking is high concept. Arnold Schwarzenegger and Danny Devito as identical twins is high concept. It's a visual image that immediately makes people smile or laugh or even shutter with the potential. When we sold *Commando,* we said, "Arnold Schwarzenegger is going to run around with a gun in his hand and kill a lot of people, and he's going to do it to rescue his daughter." That's a no-brainer.

High concept stories are plot-driven and are rarely "serious" works. It's easy to describe what high concept is by describing what it isn't.

LOW CONCEPT

Low concept movies and shows are based on drama, dialogue, and character relationships. They are not going to pitch well in a room. Largely, they are unpitchable. They may win an Academy Award, be as fabulous as *As Good As It Gets* or *Diner*. But how can you go in and pitch "seven guys in a restaurant talking"? You can't pitch it because there isn't a strong plot. You'll have nothing to talk about in the room unless you're going to read 120 pages of dialogue.

If you have a terrific story that is low concept, write the script. Send it everywhere. Hope that the right people read it. Just don't try to pitch it as an idea.

WHAT IF IT'S NEITHER-NOR?

You might have a great idea that needs more of an explanation than one or two sentences. All is not lost; it will be more difficult to sell, so keep your pitch as short as possible. Anything more than five minutes isn't short. Anything much more than ten is death. We will explain this further in the following chapters.

BACK TO HIGH CONCEPT

High concept is a cliché that is bandied about in Hollywood everyday. Everybody says they want a high concept project, but no one can ever define what a high concept movie is exactly, since no one-sentence definition exists. This is painfully ironic, since high concept movies are all about ease of explanation.

We sold a project called *Man's Best Friend*, about a genetically enhanced dog. It was a silly little thriller. We walked into the studio and said, "Imagine a poster that says: Jaws on Paws." It made everyone laugh because it's a glib rhyme and sounds cute, but it also made everyone understand that it was a scary movie about a dog. The marketability factor is very high with a high concept idea. In turn, the execs in the room who heard the pitch could explain the idea easily and succinctly. When we left the room, we knew they could sell it to the marketing division.

High concept ideas like this will begin to pitch themselves.

We walked into Warner Brothers and we said, "A sequel to the Wizard of Oz."

They said, "We don't need you for that. We own the movie, and it's the most famous movie ever made."

We gave them one sentence: "The Wicked Witch of the West didn't die but has been in Munchkin jail for fifty years and is currently in N.Y. to get the those damn red slippers." We called the movie *Surrender Dorothy, the Witch's Revenge*. Sold…in one line.

SAMPLE HIGH CONCEPT PITCH:

What do *Cinderella, Snow White,* and *Sleeping Beauty* all have in common? They are all sleeping with

Prince Charming. Now imagine Katie Holmes, Julia Stiles, and Kate Hudson, three beautiful girls, all playing fairy tale characters. Heath Ledger could be Prince Charming. The princesses are ticked off that Prince Charming has married all three of them at the same time, so they team up to teach him a lesson! Nobody ever thought about this prince being in all three fairy tales at once, which is why this idea sold to MGM.

Bob:

Be careful, though. If you can make people visualize an idea quickly, you are on your way to having a high concept idea. But *even if you make them understand your pitch quickly, it may still be a boring story.* High concepts are never boring. They may be stupid, and they may be silly, but because they are different; they are never boring. They dare to be different.

And so we've gone on and on about it (which is exactly what we said high concept ideas should never do), but just to drive the point home, here are a few more examples of high concept TV shows:

- "The Flying Nun"
- "Dennis the Menace"
- "Mork and Mindy"
- "My Two Dads"
- "I Dream of Jeannie"
- "Bewitched"
- "Gilligan's Island"
- "The Brady Bunch"

- "The Beverly Hillbillies"
- "Fantasy Island"
- "Who's the Boss?"
- "Fear Factor"
- "Who Wants to Be a Millionaire?"
- "The Bachelor"
- "Love or Money"
- "Mr. Personality"
- "Trading Spaces"
- "What Not to Wear"
- "Extreme Makeover"
- "Queer Eye For the Straight Guy"
- "The Apprentice"

Wouldn't you have loved to have come up with one or two of these ideas? And, each of these makes you pound your fist in anger and shout, "I should have thought of that! That's so obvious!"

Here is a list of high concept movies:

- *Home Alone*
- *What Women Want*
- *Bruce Almighty*
- *Jaws*
- *Jurrassic Park*
- *Cujo*
- *Mrs. Doubtfire*
- *Groundhog Day*

- *Robocop*
- *Fatal Attraction*
- *Trading Places*
- *Toy Story*
- *Big*
- *Honey, I Shrunk the Kids!*
- *Nightmare on Elm Street*
- *Freddy vs. Jason*
- *Regarding Henry*
- *Air Force One*
- *Meet the Parents*
- *Eternal Sunshine of the Spotless Mind*

Chapter 5

Start With a Good Idea

You don't have to be an original thinker; we aren't always original thinkers, either. All you have to be is someone who reads, listens, and keeps an open eye. Interesting ideas are everywhere.

So there's the good news.

Unfortunately, saleable ideas must be more than simply interesting.

FRESHNESS

Your idea must be new, original, offbeat. If it sounds at all familiar, it's probably been pitched 400 times. The last thing in the world you want to do is walk in the door with a stale, over-pitched pitch.

Of course, there are only so many basic stories: boy meets girl; boy murders boy; boy goes to war; boy comes of age; etc. How is your idea different from all the other boy meets girl movies we've seen? Is it the setting? The circumstances? Find the hook, the twist, the angle that makes your idea fresh.

"Will and Grace" is really just "I Love Lucy" with a twist. Think about it. "American Idol" is just another incarnation of "Star Search." How different are these two shows: "Everybody Loves Raymond" and "The King of Queens"? "Friends" is very similar to "Three's Company." What about "Suddenly Susan" and "The Mary Tyler Moore Show"? Though these shows bear striking resemblances to their respective counterparts, the latest versions have been updated and reflect the changing tastes of viewers. They are fresh.

If your idea is akin to a show or film of the past, use the old to justify the new:

- It's "I Love Lucy," except the Ricky character is gay and the Lucy has a career.

- It's "Star Search," but we'll only have a singing category; we'll use celebrities to comment, and viewers at home will vote. We'll get to know the contestants, interviewing them backstage.

- It's "Survivor," only with celebrities.

- It's "The Osbornes," except we'll use Anna Nicole Smith.

- It's "Jeopardy," but with bright spot lights, theater in the round, group voting, and phone calls to friends. Also, contestants can win a cool million.

- It's "The Real World," but the kids travel around, completing challenging tasks.

- It's "Love Connection," only we'll follow the couple on their date.

- It's "Blind Date," except we'll use celebrities.

- It's "Bewitched," only we'll use a teenager.

- It's "Hazel," but we'll use a male maid.

- It's "Who Wants To Marry a Millionaire?" except the women will date the bachelor for a couple of weeks. We'll catch it all on film and stretch it out for months.

- It's "The Bachelor," only with a bachelorette.

- It's "The Brady Bunch," but there's no dad, and the kids sing.

You get the idea. By building on an existing, successful concept, your pitch is abbreviated. As long as you give the idea a good, hard twist, its familiarity won't feel stale. The hook is everything. When updated, the familiar reads: fresh.

Another word of caution: Avoid linking your idea to an existing show that is ultra-super-hot. We won't even utter the words "American Idol." Too many variations of this show have been pitched, and it's become something of a joke: It's "American Idol" for sanitation engineers. The "American Idol" market has been flooded.

Die Hard is another example. The premise has been pitched in every possible way, over and over again: It's *Die Hard* in an amusement park; it's *Die Hard* in a submarine; it's *Die Hard* in Antarctica, etc.... And now we are hearing: It's *Die Hard* in a building (obviously, the setting for the original *Die Hard!*).

COMMERCIAL VIABILITY

Sadly, all the freshness in the world won't necessarily get your project made. Your idea must be seen as commercially viable as well. The entertainment industry is exactly that: an industry. It, like any other business, must sell a product and try to turn a profit.

MARKETABILITY

There is sort of a dirty, little secret in Hollywood. When you go in to pitch a story, the development people or the execs in the room don't talk about marketability. They might ask you about your characters or want to hear more details about the plot. They might even ask you about other projects you are working on. But when you leave, they will talk marketability. If they like your idea, the next question is, "How can we sell it?"

If your pitch is high concept (a simple, tight, plot-driven story), you are half way through the battle. They can toss your idea onto a poster with a title and an ad line, and the project will sell itself to the public. Home-makers will chat about it in the grocery store checkout line. It will be the topic at the office water cooler. You've made it easy for them to market your film or show, and they'll love that. The other half of the battle, how-ever, remains.

TIMELINESS

What's going on in the country, in the world right now? What is of interest to the public at large? What trends hold strong and which are waning? Read the industry trade magazines: *Variety* and *The Hollywood Reporter*. Pay attention to the ratings and box office. Watch TV and go to movies. Talk to people. Read the daily newspaper and *People*, *Cosmo*, *Sports Illustrated*, *Time*, *TV Guide*. Listen to National Public Radio.

Timeliness is easier with TV shows, since they move through development and production relatively quickly. Ideas can travel through the entire production process in a matter of months. Pitch trendy show ideas as soon as you can, for obvious reasons.

A film, however, usually takes years to write, re-write, move through development, cast, shoot, edit, and promote. A movie idea shouldn't rely upon cur-rent trends. Those trends will have long since changed when the finished product premiers. Ideas that revolve around universal themes with a fresh twist sell best.

A good example of a solid and simple idea that will stand the test of time is *Bruce Almighty*. A guy says, "I could run the world better," and God says, "Go ahead and try."

DEMOGRAPHICS

A good idea for MTV would clearly not be a good idea for The Food Network. Here again, TV differs from film.

The sheer number of cable channels has made your job of targeting production offices and studios easier. There are channels for young children, teens, middle-aged women, extreme sports enthusiasts, world travelers, Mormons, soap opera addicts, fashion watchers, game show junkies, and financial investors. If you have a show idea, there's a place to pitch it.

Of course, some of those channels are extremely specific and, accordingly, have a small viewership. A small viewership translates into a small budget.

If your show is a "reality show about day traders," you only have a couple of networks and production offices who might give you a meeting. Those networks will most likely not have oodles of money to spend on new shows. These niche channels do get shows made and put on the air, but the odds that your show will be one of the few produced in a given year are slim. Yet, if your show idea is out-of-this-world terrific, it's worth pitching it.

A fishing show meets "The Real World" will get you a few more potential meetings than the one for day traders, since this idea falls into two demographic categories: sports and travel.

A clever game show idea will get you into still more doors, since these shows fit the programming needs of many channels. They can also be syndicated and sell well internationally.

In TV, wide demographics is not necessarily the key. Knowing the potential buyer is. Research and learn all you can about a particular company and the exec before you walk through the door. By doing so, you can target buyers who want ideas like yours, and you can pitch to their specific needs. You will also save time, since you will know not to take a hot rod show to Lifetime.

In film, having an idea that appeals to a wide set of demographics is gold. For instance, lots of people like weddings, so wedding movies tend to do well. However, a film about a year in the life of a farmer will have trouble finding an audience because fewer people care about farmers and farming. Veteran filmakers will rarely produce movies that don't have wide appeal, because most film distributors will shy away from them. It comes down to money. Independent production companies are often the best bet for films with limited audience potential, and execs at these companies usually want finished scripts, not pitches.

Little by little, through the advent of the digital video age, more independent and niche market films are being made. However, they rarely turn a profit, a fact which affects how much anyone involved can be paid. Perhaps this will change in the future.

OTHER FACTORS TO CONSIDER

Castability

Will A- or B-list actors be drawn to your idea? If Julia Roberts has heard of your idea and *loves* it, it's as good as sold. Attaching talent (actors and directors) to a project can be a major selling point. Actors love juicy or unusual parts, which help them showcase their talents (think: Robin Williams in *One Hour Photo*; Jennifer Aniston in *The Good Girl*).

When formulating your idea, keep in mind specific actors as your characters. If your idea is a game show, who might host it? You might not be able to attach talent before pitching your idea to potential buyers, but referencing to specific actors in your pitch can be very helpful. It helps set the scene and can build enthusiasm on both sides. Remember that this industry (like all others) is about making money. An actor with a following generates cash.

Build strong, sympathetic protagonists—audiences need to identify with and care about your main character. Make sure he or she is endearing in some way—even if he or she is the bad guy. The protagonist also must change or grow as a result of what he goes through.

Show ideas must run several television seasons. An exec wants to know what a show will look like in its first season and its fifth season. TV shows make most of their money in syndication, when large numbers of episodes are sold to independent stations and overseas (think: "Happy Days" and "Seinfeld"). Many shows can't survive the several years required to enter the lucrative syndicated market. Make sure you know why your show will.

Conflict

Shows and films must revolve around some sort of conflict. Every story is about struggle. The main character is searching, fighting, yearning, or working to meet a goal. Without conflict, there is no story. Since stakes are relative, the inherent conflict can be as big as war (*Saving Private Ryan*) or as small as cooking a turkey (*Pieces of April*).

Structure

Stories need to have a beginning, a middle, and an end (hopefully in that order). A TV movie about vampires might be exactly what ABC is looking for, but if your idea isn't structured into a three-act storyline, the execs won't want it. This structure may change a few times as the project moves through the selling, development, and production, but it needs to be there at the time you make your pitch.

FINDING THOSE GREAT IDEAS

Bob:

I often hear people say that ideas are a dime a dozen. This is just not true. Bad ideas are a dime a dozen. Great ideas are one in a million. I liken this concept to diamond mining: You have to sift through tons and tons of rubble, but there are gems to be found. Those rare and wonderful ideas can be worth quite a lot to Hollywood, so go out and find them.

People often approach me with mundane ideas. "I have this idea for a movie about the last summer I spent with my grandmother, who died of cancer in Maine." I don't want to be rude or mean, but I am not interested in that story unless the grandmother flew around the room.

The grandmother dying is a not pitchable idea. But that's not to say there isn't a place for the story about the grandmother and her last summer in Maine. It might make a great novel or a terrific screenplay, filled will beautiful dialogue. It might even win an Academy Award. It simply can't be sold as a pitch. There is no hook. Sit down and write the script or come up with a high concept that can be pitched.

Jonathan:

I have this friend. We've known each other forever. She came to L.A. to visit me recently, and we got to talking about our terrific friendship and all of the amazing things we have been through together over the years. She said that our story would make a great movie. I had to explain that while there might be kernels of movies sprinkled here and there in our years together, as a whole, our friendship would make a boring movie. We no longer speak.

My point is this: While you may think your life is fun and fabulous, most people will not.

And, of course, we still speak.

Bob:

Has Jonathan mentioned that he used to be a comedian?

The flip side of this is that what you think of as being ordinary or pedestrian, might actually be extraordinary and interesting to others. If you can embellish or ask yourself, "what if?" and develop an intriguing story, you might generate a good idea.

Jonathan:

You look at your life. You are a dad. You notice: Teenage girls and their mothers are in a constant state of war. What if, for one long and crazy day, a daughter had to live the life of her mother and the mother had to live her the life of her daughter? Would they grow to understand each other better? Voila! You've just created a great idea. Only one problem. That's *Freaky Friday*, and it's been done. Twice, actually.

So go find another "what if." They are everywhere.

Bob:

There was a girl in my office who was attending Berkeley Law School. She mentioned something to me about a moot court case. I had never heard of such a thing. She explained that in law school students have to pick old cases, research them, and argue them in front of real judges and lawyers.

This got me to thinking. What if this girl, in researching an old murder case, stumbled upon some lost piece of evidence? What if that evidence implicated some rich, important person who had thought he'd pulled off the perfect murder ten years ago? Now, just because of this one little law student, the culprit's whole world is in jeopardy. It's a great idea. It's

Grisham. It's *Pelican Brief*. We ended up selling it to Castle Rock. She ended up getting a nice amount of money, all because she walked in and said, "moot court."

If you are in the middle of your life, just doing what you always do, you might not recognize the interesting stuff. Try to find things in your daily routine that most people don't know about. That can be the key.

Jonathan:

My old college roommate lives on a bison farm in Pennsylvania. Strangely, that's not the interesting part.

He called me in a moment of frustration, complaining about his insurance agent. He said he'd switched to a "second-to-die policy" and was annoyed at the process and the paper work. We talked for a while and said our good-byes, but after hanging up, that phrase kept banging around in my head. "Second-to-die." "Second-to-die."

I called him back and asked him just what such a policy meant. He explained that *both* parents must die before any money is paid out. Then, of course, the proceeds go to the children or to the next of kin. For the insurance company, this cuts the risk of one spouse killing the other for the money.

There was the beginning of a great thriller!

What if the wife doesn't realize it's a second-to-die policy? She and her lover plot and murder the husband, only to learn at the funeral that neither will profit—until the wife dies! So now what? Does the lover turn and kill the wife? If so, what becomes of the children?

Flesh out those questions into the basic beginning, middle, and end structure, and you might have
a blockbuster, starring Jeff Bridges, Michelle Pfeiffer,
and Sean Penn.

Bob:

Remember the movie *Double Jeopardy*, with Ash-
ley Judd? This is an example of a legal term launching
a plot that could have practically written itself. Why
did that one take so long to make?

When people find out what I do for a living, they
tend to tell me stories. I was once talking to a gynecologist at a Thanksgiving dinner who claimed to have
a good one. "Oh great," I thought. "What kind of story
is this guy going to tell me?" He prefaced it by stating
that there was a rumor going about in his hospital,
and he wasn't even sure if it was true.

A patient was suing her doctor for malpractice.
He had performed a minor surgery on her, which had
gone badly. As a result, she could never have children.
This was a boring story so far, but here was the hook:
The doctor and the patient were in on it together. They
just wanted to collect and share the insurance money.

I sold that story to CBS. It wasn't about the doctor's
daily life as a gynecologist. He'd stumbled upon this
intriguing hospital rumor, and the idea behind the rumor made a fantastic hook.

Jonathan:

That brings up an important point. When I am
listening to a pitch, I am waiting for that twist, waiting

for the other shoe to drop. The fact that the patient and her doctor were in on it together is the other shoe. Once it drops, I totally get the story.

Here's another one: There are two childhood friends. They grow up together. One becomes a lawyer and the other becomes a banker. One day, the banker approaches the lawyer about an investment opportunity. The lawyer agrees to invest one million dollars on a handshake, but he shrewdly takes out a life insurance policy on his friend.

(Hear that shoe drop?)

This way, on the off chance his dear friend should die, the money could be recouped. Of course, the investment turns out to be a scam, and the banker flees the country with the money. Now furious, the betrayed lawyer hires a hit man to kill the friend.

And that one's a true story.

Bob:

And, clearly, that's only the skeleton of the plot. Writers would be brought in to flesh it out, but that's a great setup. Completely pitchable.

There was a writer who came into my office with a simple idea the other day. Three law students lose their funding for law school due to budget cuts. They commit some sort of low-level crime on the campus to get just enough money pay for school. They are not caught. We are sympathetic to them and their plight.

Here is the hook: Six months later, one of their professors hands out the term project—the entire class must band together to solve this campus crime.

Again, there is a great setup. It needs work. The writer must figure out the twists and nuances in the plot, but you can see how that can turn into a terrific thriller.

IDEAS FROM ARTICLES, RADIO, TV

In every single magazine, currently on the newsstand, you'll find all kinds of story ideas. The articles in these magazines are important resources. The writers have done the groundwork for you. They've uncovered and interviewed and organized. Make photocopies of intriguing articles and file them for when you are brainstorming ideas.

There's a bonus with articles, too. If you walk into a studio or production office with an article, you have added credibility. Someone has already found the story interesting enough to publish it.

Watch the news. Watch talk shows. Listen to the radio. Do it regularly, daily. Focus on the stories. Ask yourself, "Is there a movie here?" Make this your mantra. Retrain your brain. Make files. Become an idea collector. In time, you'll have thousands of ideas in your files. But you must be diligent, persistent, and maybe a little bit neurotic.

Getting the rights to a story might be as simple as a phone call. Call the journalist who wrote that interesting article. Call the subject of that intriguing human interest story. Remember the "Woo-Woo Kid" story? That was optioned with a phone call. Offer the subject one dollar, one-hundred dollars, or five-hundred dollars to option the rights for a period of a year or two. During that time, you legally control the story.

You can sell it to the highest bidder, write and sell the screenplay, shoot the whole darn film. If the project yields a profit, the subject will be entitled to a pre-negotiated portion. If at the end of that time period, however, you have not exercised the option, the rights revert to the original holder. You can always re-option them for another year or two.

If the subject of a "true story" wants nothing to do with you or the film industry, you can always fictionalize the story. Use the same basic plot but change the setting and invent new characters.

IDEAS FROM BOOKS

Have you ever been reading a book and thought, "This would make a great movie"? You might be surprised to find that the subsidiary rights are available and can be purchased.

Simply look through the first few credit pages, find the name of the publishing house, and give them a call. Ask to speak to someone who handles subsidiary rights. A larger house might transfer you around a bit. In a smaller house you might find that you are talking to the sole employee and owner. Either way, ask about the availability of film rights for the book in question.

If the rights are available, explain you want to option those rights. The option may cost a few thousand dollars; it may cost one dollar. The length of the option could be several years or six months. If you are holding that option and you sell the story as a film idea, you can make that money back, and more. You'll never know unless you pursue it.

Once you hold the film rights, prepare your pitch. As with an article, a good deal of the work has been done for you. A publisher thought the story was great and invested time and money into it already. You have built-in credibility. If the book sold well, developed a cult following, or was a book club favorite—better still. Many novels and their authors have websites. Use this to your advantage and direct the buyer to the site. Let the work of others pave your way.

PUBLIC DOMAIN

Some stories are in the public domain. Public domain material is material on which the copyright has expired or material that was never copyrighted in the first place. For instance, no rights need to be obtained to pitch a movie based on *Romeo and Juliet*. If the story is 100 years old or more, you are likely safe.

WHEN LOOKING FOR AND GENERATING IDEAS, KEEP THE FOLLOWING IN MIND:

- Freshness—What's the hook, the twist?

- Marketability—Will it sell?

- Timeliness—Be mindful of trends.

- Demographics—Who is your audience and how will the audience impact the project?

- Castability—Will A- or B-list actors be drawn to your idea?

- Strong protagonist— The protagonist needs to be sympathetic and to grow or change.

- Multiple seasons—TV shows must run several seasons.

- Conflict—Stories must revolve around conflict.

- Structure—All stories must have a beginning, a middle, and an end.

Chapter 6

All-Time
Worst Pitches

We believe that by showing you some of the really bad ideas we've been pitched, you will gain a better grasp of what makes an idea good and, subsequently a saleable idea. It is important to remember that just because an idea is high-concept doesn't mean that it's necessarily good. High-concept ideas can be bad for all kinds of reasons.

GOOD EXAMPLES OF BAD IDEAS:

• *A TV Show With Gay Pachyderms as Characters.* Okay. We get the concept. It's clearly a fable. The creator's intent is probably to use the elephants as a vehicle to demystify homosexuality in a nonthreatening way. But who is the target audience? It's a cartoon, but probably not one that mainstream kids and teens will watch. But, you say, adults watch cartoons. "The Simpsons" and "King of the Hill" are examples of that. However those programs are edgy. Elephants don't convey edge. What we are left with is a show that is neither fish nor fowl. It sounds intriguing...sort of. It makes us snicker. But we cannot sell it.

In a dream world it could be produced in a dark and clever way, but it will be nearly impossible to find a producer willing to take the financial risk on such a long-shot. Find an eccentric multimillionaire, and you might be in luck. Barring that, work on your other projects.

• *Get the DNA from the Shroud of Turin and Clone Jesus.* Please, we beg of you, *don't.* This is the number one most over-pitched idea—ever. If you walk into a room with this, you will probably be stopped at the word "shroud." The origin of this pitch is probably the tired dinner party question: If you could have dinner with one person, living or dead, who would it be? Or, maybe it was the "stranded on a desert island" version. Invariably, someone will answer "Jesus" (and don't get us wrong, he's an excellent choice). This idea is so common it has become a cliché, a joke in the industry.

But here's what is interesting about this idea: Have you ever seen a movie about cloning Jesus? It begs the question: Why in the world not? It would make a great premise for a film or even a TV show. If you have an interest in writing a script, here's a story to tackle. Write the cloning Jesus story. Have at it! Just don't you dare try to sell it as an idea…we've already heard it.

• *A Talk Show for Native Americans, or a Biography Series on Native Americans.* We have nothing against Native Americans. We've put this pitch on our worst list as an example of shows with target audiences that are too small. Both could be produced in such a way that they would be compelling and educational. However, as said before, production companies want to throw their money into projects that will draw a large viewership. A show for which the primary audience is Native Americans is unlikely to do that.

Some niche markets are huge. Consider the gay community, which is estimated to comprise 11 percent of the American population. This market is hungry for programming. The last few years have created a mellowing effect on the public in regards to gay relationships. Advertisers are more likely than ever to buy airtime during and around a show like "Queer Eye For the Straight Guy" or "Boy Meets Boy." It makes financial sense to produce shows like these in the current climate.

While the Native American community is too small to support commercial development of a series, another way to get your idea produced is to apply for government grants, buy a camera, and produce it yourself. In the end, you could end up on a PBS station or showing an edited version at film festivals around the country.

But don't try to sell it as an idea.

• *An Animated Film about Bugs and Ants.* Come on. This has been done. *A Bug's Life* and *Antz* were just out a few years ago. Additionally, they were heavily promoted and overexposed in the video market. The toys, spawned by the films, are still on the store shelves. Even if you have a better storyline, what are the odds the finished film will be better? These concerns will crop up in the minds of the decision makers. It's just too soon.

If your insect storyline is fantastic, better than either *A Bug's Life* or *Antz* and you don't want to give up on it. Perhaps you should write a children's book. Or maybe a novel. After your book is published, your story will have more prestige. At that point, you can look for some one to option the rights for a screenplay.

• *Retards Say the Funniest Things.* Aside from being in bad taste, this show would never sell. There might be a huge population of folks out there who would tune in. It might even develop a cult-like following (of really, really mean people). But sponsors won't touch it.

Groups like The Association of Retarded Citizens would become enraged (and rightfully so). Advertisers who were crazy enough to have bought airtime, would back out. The show would never even air. It can't make money.

If you are dead-set on producing a show like this (and you should be ashamed of yourself), you'd better get your buddies together and do it yourself. There is probably an underground market for a show like this. But we want no part of it.

• *Man Falls For Sheep, Boy, Young Girl, Own Mother.* Okay, so the last one's been done, but if you are not a Greek-tragic playwright named Sophocles, don't even think about it. See above.

• *Eleven Contestants, Ten Parachutes...America Decides.* Here is a contest-driven reality show that involves call-in voting. These shows are hot as this book goes to press. We may be watching them for years—but probably not. The concept is just a souped-up version of the age-old dinner party question: A mother of five, a brilliant brain surgeon, and the president are on a sinking boat. Which one must be tossed overboard in order to save the other two?

The audience will get to know the characters over a period of several weeks, perhaps watch them in their home and work lives, get to know their families, and access their values as contributing members of society. These eleven people will sing, race, eat horrible, slimy foods while America watches. Each week, viewers can call toll-free from their (insert excellent product placement opportunist here) cell phone and vote for their least favorite cast member, the one they'd like to see drop dead. The final episode will be a two-hour special. America will vote and watch live, as the doomed cast member bids ado to his/her loved ones and is tossed out the cargo bay door. Fun for the whole family....

This show features many great elements: As viewers, we love to get to know the cast members, watch them interact and react. We fall in love with the "voting off" idea, to be certain, but these stakes are a smidge too high. Obviously, the public hasn't sunk so low as to vote on who lives and who dies. At least not yet.

• *Doing Time: Life On the Inside.* We follow five to seven felons from all backgrounds as they make their way through the prison system. Sounds interesting, right? As much as we'd all love to see such a show, it's too tough to sell as an idea, because it would be almost impossible to produce.

If you found a producer willing to consider this idea, he'd soon realize that shooting it would be nearly impossible. How can you get a camera crew and all of that expensive equipment into a prison? What warden in his right mind would agree to such an invasion of his cell blocks? Prisons are tightly run operations; they have to be. Filmmakers would disturb the careful balance, catch guards and prisoners in questionable acts, and generally leave a wake of chaos. Such a show or film would have to provide the audience with intimate moments and closely follow developing story threads. Hundreds of hours and months of filming would be required. The cost, the lack of access, and the enormous time, under dangerous filming conditions make this an unsaleable idea.

• *Chinese Card Game Show.* It might be an amazingly challenging and fun game to play, but what a boring, boring, boring travesty to watch. Aside from the microscopic demographics (submicroscopic, really), we are left with another insurmountable problem.

Even if the demographics were wide, game shows only work if a vast majority of the target audience completely understands and enjoys the game. Imagine the mental aerobics one would have to go through to learn even one Chinese card game. Imagine the time that would have to be devoted in each episode explain the rules.

This idea is too specific, too complicated, and too boring.

• *Walking Papers!* We watch someone get fired. The boss calls a person into the office. We watch the handing over of the pink-slip. We see him packing his office. We follow him home to see how he breaks the news to his wife and kids. He begins to search for a new job.

This is just plain sad. And, even if curiosity leads you to watch a show like this once or twice, how many destroyed lives could you stand to watch, week after week? Could there possibly be a second season? It's depressing.

Let's say you tweak the concept and you involve America. Business owners from all over the country could call and give this guy a job. This sounds uplifting, right? Sorry. Still won't work. Here, you would have one long, save-the-starving-children type of show. These shows can produce feelings of guilt in the viewer. Also, such a twist defeats the purpose of the show, which is to watch someone be miserable. How miserable would the fired person be if he knows he's going to land the best job of his life? The end product (even with careful editing) would have a fake feel.

With reality shows, fake is never a good thing.

So, Did This Help?

Keep in mind that we are all inclined to believe our own ideas are *stupendous*. And, maybe yours truly is. Hopefully, leading you through these bad pitches and explaining our reasons for condemning them has helped you to look at you own ideas with a more objective eye.

Ask yourself some tough questions and answer honestly. Step outside of your project and be your own devil's advocate; anticipate what the exec in the room might hate about your idea. If you find yourself with only a few hateful elements, all is not lost. Get back to work and make some changes. Better to do this now, in the privacy of your own world, than be shot down in a meeting with a production company.

Here's a List of Elements that Will Most Likely Make Your Idea Dead on Arrival:

- Boring to watch

- Small audience demographic

- Neither fish nor fowl (undefined audience)

- Cliché

- Too similar to a recent, successful film or show

- In poor taste

- Depressing

- Centers around culturally taboo subjects

- Too dangerous

- Too difficult

- Extremely time-consuming

- Cost prohibitive, relative to end product

- Too confusing for an audience to follow

- Reality show that generates a fake, over-edited feel

- A TV show that could never sustain a second season

Now, don't get defensive and don't just skim over the above list. Hold your idea next to each element and ask yourself how an executive in a pitch meeting might view your idea in light of that element. If need be, go back to the drawing board and see if you can fine-tune your concept. We promise that you'll be glad you did.

Chapter 7

How Much Is My Idea Worth?

A VERY TOUGH QUESTION

No. Actually it's an impossible question. And, it's impossible for many reasons, too many to list. We will give you the broad-stroke answer.

Remember your new axiom: A good idea is one in a million. Industry execs hear bad ideas (or marginally good ideas) all day long. Friends, every relative, acquaintances, and even strangers pitch them bad ideas. These people believe their ideas are fabulous and that their connection to the exec (no matter how loose) will help make them rich and famous.

Still, the execs are desperate for a one-in-a-million idea, and if you have one, they will pay for it. Just because you haven't sold an idea before doesn't mean that you have no power. You hold an idea. The idea is property, and as producer Robert Evans has said, "Property is king!" Just how much someone will pay for your idea (and in what form) varies greatly.

FORMS OF PAYMENT

Money

Money is the most obvious form of payment, but it can be structured in a myriad of ways. The buyer might pay you a lump sum, outright. You might be thrilled with $1,000. After all, now you can always say that you sold an idea to Hollywood. Depending on how well you (or your agent) negotiates and how much the buyer wants your idea, you could get anywhere from $1,000 to $100,000. The money could come to you at different stages during the life of the project. For example, upon the completion of the project, you could get a "story bonus" in the neighborhood of, say, $25,000. Or you might wind up with a percentage of the profits. Here again, we couldn't possibly list all of the different ways a deal can be structured.

Credit

In Hollywood, as elsewhere, payment doesn't necessarily mean money. Scoring an associate producer credit or a coproducer credit might be worth more to you than cash. If you are just starting out in the business, this very well may be the case. Producer credits buy you credibility. Scheduling meetings is easier if you have credits behind your name. You may even "executive produce" a project. Many of the producer titles are up for grabs, and their definitions are largely inexact. All of this can work in your favor. You might want to ask for a "created by" credit. However, don't assume this will come to you automatically (even though it seems like it should). "Created by" credit is a brass ring. It can't hurt to reach for it.

Get a Job

Take an active role. Ever want to write a script? Ask to do that. How about a job as "creative consultant"? Depending on the budget, you might even get paid for these jobs. These jobs will also get you credit.

Combine the Above

Feel free to ask for a little of everything. Remember that you own the property. It's your idea. If they want it, they will pay for it. Do, however, be reasonable with your requests. As with any negotiation, be careful not to offend the buyer. Don't ask for the moon. Be honest with yourself regarding how much your idea is worth to a particular buyer. Your price may be X, if you are dealing with a large studio, but it might be Y, if you are dealing with an independent production company.

Consider Every Angle

What if a big studio and a tiny production company are both interested? It might seem like the question leads to an obvious answer, but, alas, it does not. Large studios are huge corporations, with many captains at the helm, cooks in the kitchen, etc. Smaller, independent production companies oftentimes prove to be a smoother path toward production. The development process might not take so long. Sometimes, a movie will have a better chance of being produced and distributed by an independent (or "indie") company. What is it that you want the most? Do you want the world to see your idea up on the screen? Do you want cash? Do you want to write a script? Do you want a foot in Hollywood's door? Now, do you see why this is such a tough question for us to answer?

The Answer Is Really Up To You

If you have the following:

- a high concept idea

- done your research

- made a zillion calls

- scored many meetings in a variety of offices (gauge interest, weigh options)

- formulated, refined and practiced your pitch

- pitched your pitch well

- and found strong interest....

you are in a good position to negotiate!

Options

How does a dollar sound? Not enough? You might be surprised that optioning your idea for a dollar might not be a bad idea. If you find an independent producer or production company who wants your idea, it might offer to give you a "dollar option." The company will give you a dollar (a token which makes the deal legally binding). After you accept the dollar, the company controls the rights to your idea for a period of time. Six months to three years is common. They've leased it. In this case, your fee and/or story bonus will be paid when (and if) the project moves forward.

You can lease the option for much more than a dollar, obviously. You might require the buyer to pay you another $5,000 each time he wishes to retain the option for another six months, with a 5-year cap on how long he can continue extending the option. Or, you might score $50,000 for a two-year option. Or, you might get $72.34 in pennies. The possibilities are endless.

After the option is up, meaning it has expired, the buyer might want to renew it or "re-option" it. Of course, negotiations begin all over again. This time you might ask for more money or other conditions.

You might choose to shop the idea around, as the climate in Hollywood changes regularly. Maybe another company has been waiting for the option to expire. Perhaps the new company's interest will light a fire under the old one. Maybe there will be a bidding war over your idea.

Turnaround

If a company has bought your idea outright, the company owns it.

But wait. That's not the necessarily the end of the story. Just like any buyer of any product, the company might change its mind about the purchase. You will probably have negotiated a "no return policy," so any money you've received upfront is yours to keep. Always keep in mind that the upfront money may be the only money you will see from your idea, since projects can, and often are, stalled and shelved indefinitely.

Just like any buyer can sell his used items in a garage sale or on E-Bay, your buyer might put the project into "turnaround." If the buyer has given up on the project he will most likely want to recoup his investment. A company will have put time, money, and effort into the project. The company may have changed its mind, but that doesn't mean the company has lost anything.

Perhaps the company paid you $20,000 for your idea, spent $10,000 on early development, paid a writer $75,000 for a script, and a lawyer $25,000 in legal fees. This company will have put $130,000 into the project, and will want to sell it for that much and more—if it can. If this company is well-connected in the industry, the project will likely find a buyer.

Most times, the next buyer acquires more than your original idea. Normally, the idea, any resulting script, the legal documents, the development to-date, and the contracts with individuals, such as directors or writers, is purchased as a package.

If you have the money and the desire, you may choose to be that next buyer. After all, it's your idea and who else would care as much about it? However, if you do buy it, be wary.

Chapter 8

Protecting Your Idea

Protecting your idea is an understandable concern. What is to stop a development exec or a producer from stealing your great idea?

For the most part, these are people of integrity. Obviously, stealing ideas is bad business. Most important, personal relationships are vital in the entertainment business. Relationships within studios and between producers take years to establish. These personal and working friendships provide the opportunity to move ideas, develop entertainment properties, and produce finished products.

Because ideas are not copyrightable, the trust factor must be high. There is little tolerance for those who lack integrity. If a stolen idea results in a lawsuit against a studio, the person responsible will have doors shut in his face.

In today's litigious environment, it's less likely than ever that an idea will be stolen. Many studios and production offices are so afraid of lawsuits, they have implemented strict policies, which won't allow employees to listen to or even read unsolicited pitches. Mailed and faxed pitches will often go straight into the trash can. These fears protect you.

That being said, telling your idea to anyone is still a risk. If you are not comfortable taking that risk, please do not do so. But, of course, if you don't tell someone your idea, you will never sell it.

There are several ways you can protect your idea so that you will feel more comfortable when pitching it.

REGISTER YOUR TREATMENT

Your treatment (See Chapter 9 for information on how to prepare a treatment.) should be registered with the Writers' Guild of America (WGA) as soon as possible. You can mail it, e-mail it, or hand-carry it. At the time of this writing, the cost for this registration is a mere twenty dollars and may protect you and your idea down the road. You may also register scripts, synopses, outlines, written ideas for TV or radio, video cassettes/disks, and interactive media. The association also accept plays, novels, nonfiction books, short fiction, poems, commercials, lyrics, and even drawings. The WGA cannot protect titles. The WGA is an invaluable resource for writers. For extra protection register your treatment, outline, or synopsis of work with the copyright office. (See "Resources" for contact information for the WGA or the copyright office.)

Bob:

Don't worry if the treatment isn't perfect. Just write it out like a sixth-grade book report with a beginning, middle, and end.

If you pitch your idea and later find someone else working on it, you will have the dated registration certificate. Therefore, you have a good start for a lawsuit.

Remember, if you have a fabulous, specific idea, 99 percent of the time an interested party will not steal it; the party will offer to pay you for it.

Jonathan:

It's later, in contract negotiations, that you want to be wary. A buyer may try to belittle your contribution or take financial advantage of you. Be respectful, but be firm about what you are due.

MAIL IT TO YOURSELF

This might seem like overkill, and it is. But it can't hurt. Your idea in a postmarked, unopened envelope, tucked safely away in a drawer might help you sleep at night.

Jonathan:

You can also bury it in your back yard in a time capsule, which can be carbon dated at a later time by a team of scientists.

Bob:

OK, now we're getting a bit overboard, and don't bury it. Just don't die from worry that someone will steal it.

BE MINDFUL

When practicing your pitch in Omaha, feel free to use strangers, like the waiter at the Red Lobster, your cab driver, the local mortician. Have at it.

But, in L.A. even the mortician could be an out-of-work actor, producer-to-be, or in film school at night. Since the best ideas are high concept and simple, they travel well. They spread and become part of the L.A. ether and suddenly, BAM!, you read about it in *The Hollywood Reporter* and say, "Hey! That was my idea!" Sadly, that's just part of the business.

BE CONCISE AND SPECIFIC

The higher the concept, the tighter the pitch and the catchier your logline (the phrase used to give the flavor of the idea, for example, "Jaws on Paws"), the safer you'll be. It's risky to steal a very specific idea. If you walk into meetings with a general idea ("It's a love story aboard the Titanic"), you are doing nothing more than suggesting a broad topic, or perhaps fueling an interest in other Titanic projects in development. An idea that general is impossible to protect. If, however, you tell the story about this guy named Jack and this girl named Rose and you explain how the film will be done in flashback and Jack dies, etc., it becomes more than just a loose idea about the Titanic and turns into a recognizable and traceable concept.

Quickly map an intriguing storyline and concisely introduce compelling characters. Repeat your logline several times while in the room.

PITCH IT EVERYWHERE

Once you start to pitch your idea, get into as many offices as quickly as you can, so you your name will be linked with your idea.

Chapter 9

Preparing Your Pitch

You have a solid idea. You are just about to make dozens of phone calls, which will result in a handful of scheduled and potential meetings. You have been pitching your idea to your friends and family. Your dog has heard it three times a day. In the shower, while driving to work, on dates, during your workout, you have pitched this idea. Each time you pitch it, you refine and polish it. You think it is the best idea—ever. Let's make sure you are on the right track. Here's how to get your pitch meeting-ready and meeting-worthy.

TITLES

Give your project a working title, with the understanding that even the most masterful, most brilliant title will change many times throughout the life of a project. Choose memorable words that convey your concept. A fabulous title often can serve as a pitch.

- "Who Wants to be a Millionaire?"

- "Mr. Personality"

- "Sex and the City"

- "Average Joe"

- "NYPD Blue"

- "Friends"

- "That 70s Show"

- *The Last Samurai*

- *Heat*

- *My Big Fat Greek Wedding*

ANATOMY OF A PITCH

Once in the room, the general rule to follow is to aim for five minutes. You want the whole meeting to last no longer than ten minutes, max.

Open with your high concept. "It's a TV show idea: 'Candid Camera' meets *Pay It Forward*." As mentioned, formulating the perfect high concept is a challenge. Put ample time and thought into it, as this can make or break your meeting. It can sell your idea or kill it.

The above high concept was all that was needed to sell the show "Good Samaritan" to Disney. No further pitch was needed. The exec got the concept immediately and bought it in the room.

Bob:

This is the test, folks: Can you put your whole idea into one or two sentences? If not, it's going to be tough to sell.

If a concept is simple, fresh, and has an interesting hook, it will "have legs." It will pitch itself; it will travel the hallways of the studio. It will stand on its own. Soon your phone will ring and you'll be called in to sign the contracts.

However, your high concept alone might not result in an immediate sale. You must be prepared to elaborate the idea. Succinctly explain the beginning, the middle, and the end—adding color.

Sometimes an idea cannot be easily compressed. Try as you might, you can't boil it down. You find you need to explain the hook, or maybe your characters are so intriguing that they *are* the concept and so they must be described. Now your job is more difficult, but all is not lost. Your pitch will be longer, yet it is still of extreme importance to keep it as tight as possible to keep the attention of your exec.

FILM TREATMENTS

So, how do you prepare to take a complex movie idea and present it in ten minutes or less? Start by writing out your entire idea. This document is called a treatment.

Writing a treatment forces you to flesh out, examine, and explore your idea. Such an exercise might prompt you to kill off characters or change the plot in its entirety.

You hear a lot about treatments in this business. They are only valuable for two reasons: registering your idea with the Writers' Guild and working out your pitch. While it is common for execs to ask for a copy of your treatment, we believe it is rarely a good idea to leave a treatment with the exec after a meeting. We feel it is better to leave the exec with a tantalizing one or two-sentence high concept. But this is only our opinion, and there are plenty of folks who will disagree.

For those of you who want to use your treatment as a "leave-behind," here are some simple rules. Make every sentence count—load each one with lots of information, shoot for a high ratio of ideas to words. Write in the present tense. Use highly-visual, colorful language. Keep it short. These are good rules to follow, even if no one except you ever sees your treatment.

At first pass, you might fill twenty pages or more with a film treatment. This is not a pitch; this is a novelette. It is good for you to have fleshed out the concept into a story, but now you must get back to work. Cut the treatment down to the barest essentials. Got five pages? Still too long for many busy execs. Try to shrink it down to two pages. It may seem impossible, but try. It's not the end of the world if you walk into a room with five or even seven pages, as some stories simply need more details than others. Brevity is best, but not if you must sacrifice imperative information.

A treatment for a film should include the following:

- A working title

- Your name and contact information

- WGA registration number

- The one or two-sentence high concept logline

- An introduction to the important characters

- The setting (only if important to the story)

- Beginning (Act I): Sets the scene. conflict is introduced

- Middle (Act II): The heart of the story, usually contains the climactic moment

- End (Act III): Conflict is quickly resolved, characters have changed

Your treatment (especially if it is to be used as a "leave-behind") must generate empathy for the characters, show the flavor of the dialogue, and capture the very spirit of the movie. Above all, understand that without conflict, you have no story. Conflict is the basic building block of drama. Think: struggle, desire, obstacles, yearning.

Add color by briefly describing important setting aspects and inserting vivid scenes like car chases or exploding buildings. These scenes build drama and tension. They provide release and help establish character. Descriptive bursts help play the movie in the head of the listener. We all can visualize what a torrential flood scene looks and feels like. We know the smells and vibrations of recess at an elementary school in the late spring. With very few words, you can invoke vivid and moving images in the mind of the listener. But beware, too many vivid images could invoke numbness in the listener. Choose and use them wisely.

REALITY SHOW TREATMENTS

A treatment for any TV show is different from a film treatment . Shows are episodic, so they don't have one, long, traditional storyline. Instead, each episode is like a short film. The pilot establishes the world of the show, and subsequent episodes are like sequels. You need to set up the world, introduce it's characters, and explain what viewers will see in each episode.

A thorough "leave-behind" treatment for a reality show should include the following:

- The working title

- Your name, WGA registration number, and contact information

- The high concept

- Background on the concept

- Basic character types

- Episode one (three acts)

- Episode two (three acts)

- Episode three (three acts)

- Continue for several more episodes...

- The finale, big "payoff" episode (three acts)

- A brief explaination of what the next four seasons will look like

It is not necessary to compile the above items into a glossy, three-ring binder. As we have mentioned, you might choose to not leave anything behind at all. However, if you haven't worked through this information, your idea may seem incomplete. The exec might ask questions, and you might not know the answers.

Of course, you can't possibly know exactly what will happen on reality TV, which is why it has become the darling of prime time. Understand that a reality show is not a documentary. It is a finely-crafted, highly-edited, episodic series, using real people in interesting situations and settings.

Just be sure to get the high concept with the approximate arc of the season in your treatment. As with any TV show, each episode is a micro-movie and must have a beginning, middle, and end. At the same time, each episode builds upon the last, moving the lead and recurring characters through the larger plot. Formulating these micro-movies will be tough. You must invent participants and create many intricate possible storylines.

It is frustrating that the minute the show is cast with real people, all of your stories will probably disappear. It may seem pointless, but without this effort your show won't sell as easily. You can always use the characters and storylines in another project, since you (we hope) have lists and lists of them.

Remember that the concept might be easily explained, but the stories and characters won't be. Spend a great deal of time working this out and condensing it.

TREATMENTS FOR GAME SHOWS

For a game show, you will include in your treatment the high concept and the description of the game. However, game shows can be as tricky to describe as tying a shoelace with your tongue. Can you imagine the pitch for "The Price Is Right"? Most game shows have multiple components: side games, tie breakers, lightning rounds. Spend a good deal of time refining your show, whittling it down to is most basic elements. Be sure to pick colorful verbs to describe the action and drama of the competition. As with any show you create, be prepared to watch it morph into a very different show, once it is sold.

TREATMENTS FOR HYBRID SHOWS: COMPETITIVE REALITY SHOWS

As we are sure you have noticed, most reality shows have a game show component. The competitors, who are really the characters in the drama of the show, are all trying to win the million dollars, the handsome bachelor, etc. These shows will require special handling, since you must describe both the competition and the estimated arc of the plot. Most likely, you will not be able to fit this onto a page (or even two pages). It's understandable. Likewise, these shows can require a more lengthy pitch. If it's a good enough idea, the longer pitch will still hold an interested exec's attention. Currently, these shows sell quickly, as they are in great demand. By the time you are reading this, the reality boom might be over.

TREATMENTS FOR DOCUMENTARY/BIOGRAPHY SHOWS

The success of shows like "Wild On!," "Good Eats," "True Life," "A and E's Biography," and "The Crocodile Hunter" proves that television audiences enjoy learning from—and not just being entertained by—TV. The new high-definition networks are searching for this kind of programming, and these types of shows are currently selling well. Expect a sustained interest in cooking shows, travel shows, home remodeling shows, and the like.

Start with the working title. State the high concept. Give a brief background on the subject (history, statistics, the public's level of interest, etc.). List dozens of potential subjects/topics, expressing one-sentence interest level for each. Be sure that you are prepared to talk about several of these subjects in-depth, if asked.

TREATMENTS FOR SOAP OPERAS

Forget soap operas. The market is flooded.

TREATMENTS FOR NEWS MAGAZINES AND TALKSHOWS

These aren't really pitchable, since they are talent dependent. However, if, for some reason, you can bring the talent to the table....

TREATMENTS FOR DRAMAS AND SITCOMS: "BIBLES"

Creating and selling a drama or sitcom series is a lofty goal. The big studios have scores of in-house writers, all trying to do the same thing. Largely, these series are talent-dependent. *It's a hospital drama, starring Meatloaf. It's a Steven Bochco cop show. It's a family sitcom, and Adam Sandler is the dad.* You probably don't have access to these people (yet).

In this extremely competitive field, your show will be difficult to sell. Even getting meetings will be more difficult. If your series idea is the edgiest and most innovative property imaginable, it might be worth a shot.

Creating a series treatment, a "bible," is like building a world. Preparation is formal, labor intensive, and time consuming. It should include the following:

- Your name, WGA registration number, and contact information

- A working title

- A knock-your-socks-off high concept

- A synopsis for the pilot episode

- A one-sheet, briefly describing all of the major characters

- A one-sheet per major character analysis, providing an in-depth description

- A one-sheet on the *franchise* (the unique setting or situation) of the show—i.e., the bar on "Cheers," the cruise liner on "The Love Boat," the traveling world of the angels on "Touched By an Angel"

- Background research on the subject, when needed—i.e., information on the "multiverse" for "Sliders," the history of Area 51 and the alien-watcher/abduction theory subculture for "X Files."

- A treatment for the pilot

• Synopses for six to twelve future episodes

And, you'll need the glossy binder this time. Think: formal business plan.

REFINING THE PITCH

After you have your treatment perfected, create a one-sheet or, better yet, a one paragraph version of it. Make it your goal to condense the whole project into less than one page. This might seem like an insurmountable task. Doing so will require you to describe only the most essential components.

With movies, you'll likely have to introduce fewer characters and record only the key moments that move the plot along. For TV shows, create an outline that highlights only the most important points.

Read your one-sheet aloud. Get your friends to read it. Does it capture everything you need to convey? If not, get back to work.

Bob:

Just to clarify: We don't suggest bringing your treatment or one-sheet to a pitch meeting, and you certainly shouldn't read aloud from it. We don't like leaving anything behind in the room. We get in, pitch, and leave. Handing something over in print might discourage a sale. The value of the one-sheet is that it forces you to be concise.

Use your one-sheet to form and refine your pitch. That doesn't mean memorize it. Repeating the plot over and over can be a bit dangerous. You don't want it to sound memorized. Enthusiasm and spontaneity is essential when pitching.

Chapter 10

Getting into the Room

You have a great idea and a well-formulated pitch. You've registered your treatment with the Writers' Guild and the copyright office. You are all set. So now, go out and get some meetings. Even if you don't live anywhere near L.A., you can do this. Honest.

Jonathan:
You cannot be afraid to pick up a phone.

When I was in commercial real estate, my boss came into my office one day and found me pushing around papers. I was just killing time, and he knew it.

His response was great advice, which I've never forgotten.

"Jonathan," he said. "You can do whatever you want, or you can pick up the phone and make money."

I am now a cold-call fanatic. I will cold-call any one and everyone that I feel is necessary to consummate a mutually beneficial deal. You must pick up the phone and call and call and call. Don't stop calling. Be relentless in your fight for your idea!

Bob:

You get on the phone and call every vice president of development and every creative director in town. You call, fax, and e-mail with an obsessive, neurotic focus. Everyone else is obsessive and compulsive, so you'd better be too.

WHERE TO BEGIN?

Go online and subscribe to or buy a copy of *The Hollywood Creative Directory* or *The Producers' 411*. This isn't optional. You must have one of these guides.

Either will do, but *The Hollywood Creative Directory* is updated three times a year, while *The Producers' 411* is updated once a year. Both publications contain hundreds of companies' specialty areas, key executives, contact information, credits, guild affiliations, etc. This information will help you decide where your idea might sell and which exec to contact. *The Producers' 411* has a wonderful free website (www.411publishing.com), but it lacks much of the information you will need.

You have probably never heard of most of the small companies listed in these guides and might be tempted to avoid them. This would be a mistake. Small, independent producers, agents, entertainment attorneys, and writers' managers can be quite helpful in getting you and your project into a big studio. These Hollywood insiders have established connections with other industry professionals. They can take your idea (or the whole treatment, if you prefer) and pitch it for or with you. Their credibility adds to the weight of your project, and it will be heard in a greater number of offices. They will take a cut of the deal, but after your first sale, *your* credibility will have grown. Pitch your idea to *every* and *any* office who could possibly be interested. This partnering path might be the easiest and the most profitable way to get into the market for a newcomer.

Jonathan:

Don't work harder. Just work smarter.

If you have an idea for a game show, simply flip to the television production office section. There you will find contact information for offices like Fremantle, which primarily focuses on foreign and domestic game shows (they brought "American Idol" to Fox). And don't shy away from contacting Fox, CBS, or one of the other networks directly. You have all of the information right in front of you. Use it.

So You've Got a Good Idea, a Pitch, and the Numbers to Call: Now What?

Jonathan:

Producers have set up a screening process, designed to keep you out.

Don't panic. Obviously, the most persistent people with the best ideas make it through the process and go on to sell their ideas. To be one of those folks, you must prove to the assistant that your idea must be heard.

If my assistant asks me to read something or do something, I don't even bother to ask why. I just do it. There is a level of trust and confidence with an assistant, and there has to be. As producers, we are thrown an extraordinary amount of information every hour of the day. We rely upon our assistants to sift through that information, screen and return phone calls, read scripts, and a thousand other things. Truly, these people are not really assistants, they are right arms. They are lifelines.

So you see where this is going. When you start to make phone calls, record the name of every assistant. Even if the assistant tells you the boss is terribly busy and has no time for pitches—ask for and write down the assistant's name! If you've been so lucky as to have struck up a conversation with an assistant, write down exactly what you've talked about and when. The next time you contact the office, you will be able to communicate on a more personal level.

If you weren't fortunate enough to visit with the assistant, just knowing her name can be enormously helpful. "Julie! Hi, it's Pete over at Phantom Entertainment. Does he have time for a fifteen-minute meeting today? I am going to be in the area."

It's not rocket science. It's just being nice. This business involves teaming with all types of personalities. Use this to your advantage by being kind and thoughtful.

Bob:

I try to get my idea into the offices anyway that I can. I will use faxes and e-mail. But you do have to be careful and protect your idea. Giving away too much is an obvious mistake. Instead of sending a treatment (or even a paragraph), I will send an interest-generating logline, like "Jaws on Paws."

Remember the movie, *Alien*? The logline was, "In space, nobody can hear you scream." That sort of line is going to grab attention.

Remember that you are not a nobody. You own an idea, and with an idea you are a somebody.

Jonathan:

I am not a fan of the expression, "It's not what you know; it's who you know." In fact, I vehemently disagree with it. Get out there. Get meetings. Begin to work on projects and forge relationships. If you are reliable and personable, your good work will automatically cultivate new friendships and foster trust. Before you know it, they'll be only one or two degrees of separation between you and nearly everyone in the industry.

Do not blame failure on lack of connections. Go and make connections. Start with a couple hundred phone calls.

IF YOU DON'T LIVE IN L.A.

Living in Nebraska or Mississippi will add challenges to your quest for meetings, but it doesn't make it impossible.

Airfare and hotel prices are extremely low, using Internet sites like Hotwire and Travelocity, and no matter where you live, L.A. is only a few hours by plane. Rental cars can be obtained for under twenty-five dollars a day. A three-day trip can cost under $400. Does that seem like a lot of money? What if you are able to schedule eight or ten meetings in those days? What if you make that trip four or five times a year?

If you absolutely love living in Nebraska, stay put, and just commute. You might eventually decide to make the move to Tinseltown, but until then—just think how much money you'll save in living expenses.

Jonathan:

A word of caution: If you live out of state, never let the assistant or the exec think that you are flying in to see him exclusively (even if you are). This is far too much pressure to put on him. Suddenly your no-nonsense fifteen-minute meeting mutates into a large obligation on his part. Pitch meetings are probably not a top priority for him and many times must be postponed. Since he will not be able to guarantee the pitch meeting, he might find it safer to say no than to be responsible for your flying 1,000 miles to California for naught.

Just frame your request like this: "I will be in your area on May 3 and 4 and would love to swing by for fifteen minutes." Be sure to leave a cell number with the assistant in case the meeting time must be moved or cancelled. Set up as many meetings as you can. If one or two are cancelled, your travel expenses and time won't have been wasted.

Chapter 11

Once You Are In the Room

The following are some imperative do's and don'ts once you find yourself "in the room."

THE DO'S:

Do Be On Time

This may seem obvious and not worth a mention, but we feel that we must caution you here. If you do not live in the Los Angeles area, you are probably unfamiliar with its sometimes rhythmic, sometimes chaotic, sometimes standstill traffic patterns. A five-mile journey might take you five and a half minutes, or it might take five and a half hours. Something as simple as few drops of rain can slow perfectly decent traffic to an excruciatingly slow crawl.

Buy a copy of the Los Angeles area *Thomas Guide*. This beefy, detailed book of street maps should be riding shotgun in your car. Within its pages, you will find ways to cut through the freeway system. Find it online or buy it when you get to town. Set your car radio to a station that broadcasts traffic every few minutes. AM stations 980 and 1070 can save you valuable time.

Clearly, it's always a good idea to allow for extra time to get to your appointment. If you arrive early, run through your pitch, call to confirm other meetings, grab a coffee. If you are running late, you must call the office. Let the assistant know that you will be late and give her an approximate arrival time.

But, please, do everything in your power to be on time. Remember that the producers and the execs with whom you're meeting are phenomenally busy. By being late, you risk messing with their schedules. They might cancel the meeting entirely. Next time you call to request a meeting, they might turn you down flat.

The other side of the coin is that producers and execs are often running behind. Yes, we see the irony. You can not be late, but they can be. That's just the way it goes. Since you know this, never schedule your meetings too close together in time. Likewise, don't schedule them too far apart in geographical distance. Leave lots of room for cushion. Back-to-back meetings at Disney, in Burbank, and at CBS, near Mid-Wilshire, should be avoided. Use the *Thomas Guide* to help you map your day.

Do Sign the "Studio Release Agreement"

The Studio Release Agreement is a document that you might be asked to sign. Sign it. It's become somewhat of a standard in the industry, due to our hyper-litigious society. It states that you agree to not sue the company if they end up producing a film or show, which resembles yours.

Wait! Don't panic.

Your knee-jerk response to a legally binding document like this is probably shock and horror. We don't blame you. The agreement is a necessary evil for the studios. Lawsuits are as expensive as they are annoying. They require vast amounts of time, effort, money, and emotion. Nobody wants them. This document discourages such suits.

If a company steals your idea, you can still sue it. It's possible to sue anyone for anything, after all.

Try to step into the shoes of a studio. For example: Fox produced and released the film, *Ice Age*. Let's pretend that Peter Pitcher had pitched the execs at Fox an idea for a film about people surviving in the ice age. Now Peter is angry. He feels Fox took his idea and didn't pay him for it. He wants to sue. Never mind that *Ice Age* is an animated children's film with talking animals and Peter's is a romantic adventure story. Peter still thinks that Fox took his idea, and he will make Fox pay!

There are hundreds of Peters out there, and Fox knows this. The people there hope that by having Peter (and pitchers like Peter) sign such an agreement, he will think long and hard before contacting a lawyer. They hope that he will abandon the idea of a lawsuit completely. Peter is angry, but Peter has no case. His idea had the same backdrop as Fox's film, but the similarities end there.

Fox would win the suit, but the company would lose time, money, and effort. Studios and production companies simply must discourage frivolous lawsuits.

In the end, the agreement helps pitchmen. It allows the studios to listen to and consider our ideas. Without such a document, they might all just choose to generate ideas for their projects internally.

Do Show That You Are Aware of Current Projects and Past Successes

Research the studios and production companies you'll be contacting. Know their past and current projects; learn what is slated for production in the near future. Use your research to illustrate how your idea fits into a particular company's format, goals, and timing. Being able to discuss this demonstrates to an exec you are professional enough to have done the proper research, that you feel your idea is a good fit for his company, and that you aren't just shooting blind.

A word of caution: Don't be preachy. Let MTV execs know your idea fits their demographics, but don't tell them their demographics are 12- to 22-year-olds. They know.

Bob:

I go into a room with a list of ideas. I like to be prepared to give the execs what they need if the opportunity presents itself. Maybe I will pitch one or two ideas, or maybe I will give them more. I've worked with these people for years. They know that the ideas on my list will be commercial, at the very least. They are usually willing to listen to several ideas, since I keep them short..

The more I pitch, the more I sell.

Jonathan:

I like to approach the execs with one or two ideas at a time. I want them to know that I have weeded through all of my ideas, and have selected the perfect projects for them. However, execs often ask for more. In which case, I am happy to provide more.

Do Be Enthusiastic

You believe in your idea. You know it's going to make everyone involved a boatload of cash. Make sure everyone in the room understands this. Convey an air of excitement about your project. If you aren't thrilled with it, how can they possibly be? Your enthusiasm will fuel theirs. It's infectious.

Maintain eye contact. Smile. Enjoy your story as you tell it.

Do Read the Room

At the same time, gauge the energy level in the room. If everyone else is calm and quiet and low-key but you are jumping around the room, you could come off looking like a circus performer. If this is the case, you won't appear enthusiastic...just kind of creepy.

Again, maintain eye contact. Talk to these people, not at them. You are confiding in them, not pontificating to them. Notice their body language. Are they open and attentive, or are they only marginally aware of your existence?

Maybe they are tired or hungry. Maybe the biggest deal they ever landed just went belly-up. Maybe they just aren't in the mood. If they seem unreceptive, you might need to dial your pitch down.

Conversely, if they are rolling with laughter and are thoroughly entertained by your pitch, run with that. Take advantage of the high energy and give your idea the hard sell.

Do Be Confident

You've done your research and you know exactly with whom you are meeting. You know what they've produced in the past and the types of projects they are looking to aquire. And you have an idea with legs!

Do Be Brief

You may be sick of hearing this, but it bears repeating. Pitch, thank them, and get out. This brevity will read: I respect your time. It will also convey that you are busy and have other meetings (which, of course, you do). Any lingering or small talk might damage your chances for future meetings. Keep in mind that you are building relationships. Always leave the room on an up note.

Do Allow For Collaboration

As you begin to pitch, the execs will listen. At a certain point in your pitch, they will "get" the concept and see where the plot or show is going. Once they get it, they will most likely stop listening and start working through the idea in their minds. They think about commercial viability, timing, demographics, their other shows, how they will pitch your idea "up the ladder." That glazed look might not mean that they are bored. It could, in fact, be a very good thing.

They might start to throw out ideas of their own, tweaking your idea. Stress not. This is okay. Truly, you want this. If they are personally vested in the idea, their enthusiasm for it will grow. If they are enthusiastic, they will try harder to sell the idea to their higher-ups.

This may sound a bit sinister or Machiavellian, but maintaining a collaborative spirit can get you a development deal. After all, the execs know better than you what their company is looking to buy.

They might ask you leading questions. "And does the terrible antagonist die a horrific, bloody death?" "Should the girl dump him for her professor?" They might put a great, new spin on the idea.

Be willing to morph your plot a bit. This doesn't mean you should completely abandon your original idea. Just aim to be the easiest person in the room.

Flexibility is always an asset. Be open to another's thoughts. You may even like the revised idea better.

Sure, an exec might take some of the credit, but you are the creator. Leave this to be negotiated later.

THE DON'TS

Don't Panic

Yes, the execs to whom you are pitching could launch your ideal career and lead you to wealth beyond your wildest dreams. Odds are they won't, but the thought that they could is a bit unnerving. Do not panic. Everyone in that room is in the business of making money. They want to succeed. They want your idea to be fantastic, so they can get rich and famous—or richer and more famous.

Sure, they might ask you some tough questions about your idea, playing devil's advocate, looking to ferret out major holes in your idea. Don't be alarmed by this. You've asked these same questions while preparing this pitch (and if you haven't, then get back to the drawing board). It is their place to pick your concept apart and look at it from every angle. View this kind of probing as a compliment. If your idea weren't intriguing, they would quickly thank you and dismiss you.

Don't Initiate Small Talk

Every meeting needs a little warm-up, or an ice-breaking moment, but please remember that the execs are busy. They want to hear about your idea. They do not care about what a beautiful day it is outside or how you were caught in three accidents on the freeway. Get in there and get to the pitch.

Don't Rush

While it is important to keep your meeting as brief as possible, never rush through your pitch. Nervous energy will often cause pitchers to move through the necessary information far too quickly. Vital points in the pitch might be glossed over or dropped completely. Suddenly, the pitch that you worked and reworked makes no sense. Additionally, the increased speed can make it tough for those listening to hear and understand all of your words.

Plan ahead for this. Time your pitch so that you will feel comfortable with its natural length and not feel the need to hurry through it. Practicing the pitch in front of strangers (the waiter, your doctor, your kid's soccer coach) will be helpful. You'll be surprised by how receptive people are to hearing ideas for Hollywood. Take the edge off of the fear before your meetings begin.

When in the room, remember to keep your wits about you. Keep eye contact. Carefully and clearly tell these people your idea.

Don't Oversell

An interesting problem could arise when an exec has to pitch your idea up the ladder to his superiors. He may not be as skillful at pitching this particular idea as you—after all it's your idea and no one is likely to be as enthusiastic as you are. The initial dazzle may be lost in the translation. If the idea is shot down, the exec maybe annoyed and embarrassed.

If you have to work too hard convincing the exec, the idea probably won't sell up the ladder. If the idea doesn't have legs, it cannot stand on its own. The best pitching in the world can't sell it.

Don't Talk Your Way Out of a Sale

If they love your idea and want to buy it, take yes for an answer. The sale ends when the customer says "yes." At that point, stop talking and get out of the room as quickly as possible. You never know what might change their minds, so go home. Celebrate.

Jonathan:

We once sold a show but had made the mistake of bringing its talkative creator to the meeting with us. After a fantastic pitch and an immediate offer to buy the concept, our guest felt compelled to start chatting. He began to explain his reasons for creating the idea, a TV show that lampooned all court shows. He went on to state the reasons that court shows were so bad and deserving of ridicule. He went on and on and on.

After several minutes of this, the execs began to squirm. Their network was currently airing several of these shows and they started to wonder if it was a good idea to make fun of their own shows. What had been a fabulous idea, only moments before, now seemed horrible. They backed out of the sale.

Once they love it, leave!

Don't Leave Material Behind

As we mentioned before, we typically don't leave written material behind.

When we leave the room, we want to be sure that all of the questions have been asked and answered. We hope we have covered all of the reasons the idea is fabulous. If an exec wants further information, he can contact us.

The last thing we'd want is for him to sit alone, reading over our idea.

The energy in a live pitch brings a concept to life in a way that printed words on a page cannot. The exec could be thrilled with the idea, then go back and reread it before pitching it up the ladder and find it not nearly as exciting as he remembered.

Or perhaps, while reading it, he comes up with reasons the show or film might not work. If we are not there to work with him, answer his questions, and explain away his concerns, the idea could be abandoned.

Having stated and restated our position on leave behinds, nothing is set in stone. You will find that some buyers will ask for a one-page treatment. If you say you do not have one with you, some execs will request that you get one to him. In these instances, send it.

Don't Become Discouraged

You might pitch an idea for the first time and make a sale. You might pitch it ten or twenty times before someone shows interest. In this business it is easy to feel your confidence slipping away. This loss of confidence can only hurt your chances of a sale. If you have a solid, commercially viable, high concept idea, and you have a concise, enthusiastic pitch…eventually, you will find a buyer.

Do not stop! Be relentless.

Chapter 12

Staying Cool In Development Hell

This chapter will explain one of those disappointing facts of life: the development process. Repeat after us: Life isn't fair.

WHAT IS DEVELOPMENT?

Once an idea has been sold, it moves into the development phase. It is at this point that movie scripts are written and rewritten. TV shows change formats, sometimes so vigorously that the end product looks nothing like the original idea. Talent (actors and directors) are attached and unattached. The project moves from the front burner to the back burner to the front burner, again and again. *Shakespeare in Love* sat on the shelf at Universal for ten years before it was produced. Most people are shocked to hear things like this, but it's a typical scenario.

WHY DOES IT TAKE SO LONG?

There are a thousand and one reasons. The following are some possible scenarios:

- Let's say you sold an idea to Miramax. Maybe Jennifer Aniston was toying with the lead role, which led to Spielberg showing interest. The project was handed over to a hot writing team. The whole town is now abuzz. But—alas! Jennifer decides against moving forward. Without her, Spielberg bows out. Without A-list talent attached, the hot writing team focuses its attention on another script. The studio, which holds the option, lets the project sit a spell. This spell can be ten years or longer.

- You optioned your idea to Fox for three years. No big-deal talent had been attached, but the exec loved, loved, loved it. You were wooed by her enthusiasm and were sure that it would swiftly move through development and earn you that $75,000 story bonus within a year. Before this could happen, your exec became pregnant and took a year off. She returned to work, but as a new mom, she wasn't so gung-ho on your violent film about a serial-killing clown. You lunch with her a few times, trying to refuel her earlier interest and nearly pull it off, but she suddenly leaves Fox for a higher-ranking position at Universal. Her replacement worked his way through college as a party clown and hate, hate, hates the project. You decide to sit quietly and allow the three years to pass. Meanwhile, you mentally gear up to shop it around when the option expires and the project reverts back to you, but Fox decides to re-option it. You are beaten down by this whole process and chose the path of least resistance: You take another three years at Fox.

• Let's say you sell a game show to a production company. The execs are giddy about the idea and bought it before you could finish your pitch. You were even able to negotiate a co-producer credit. But they found that the show would be too expensive to produce and shelved it. You ask to buy your idea back, in hopes of selling it elsewhere. They refuse, not wanting to hand their competitors a hit show. You offer them even more money. They won't budge.

Finally this production company decides to put your idea into "turnaround." You want to buy it back, but there is a bidding war and your pockets aren't as deep as another production company's. This company, in turn, gets busy with another project and places your idea on the back burner. Sure, if your show ever gets made, you'll still get coproducer credit, since it's in the original agreement, but, after the years pass, you may end up bragging about it to your fellow residents in the old folk's home.

We told you. Life isn't fair. In all of this passing time, you feel you should have become the next new thing! The toast of the town! You should have walked down the red carpet on the night of the splashy premiere. That film should have launched your career, and you should have been living in the Hollywood Hills for nearly a decade. But again, life isn't fair. There are thousands of reasons for projects being stalled or killed in development and only a few ways a project can be produced.

WHAT'S THE POINT?

We know. It looks bleak. How does one survive development hell? We suggest what might be (for you) the impossible: Once sold, forget about it. Really. Take the money, negotiate credit, and maybe a story bonus, then get out. Don't look back.

Move on to the next idea. You're creative, develop scores and scores of hot, new ideas. If you have twenty projects in development, your odds are pretty good for getting one produced. Meanwhile, you can say, "I currently have twenty shows in development." This statement lends you credibility and could help you get more meetings and sell more ideas.

Bob:

I like to use the image of the myth of Sisyphus.

Knowing that there is no harsher punishment than that of useless and futile labor, the gods ordered Sisyphus to endlessly roll a huge rock up to the top of a mountain, at which point, it would roll back down. Picture this guy, all straining and sweaty. He struggles to move this rock because he must. He is compelled to do this. When that rock rolls down, he's got to follow it and start over. What does he think about during his descent? He knows it's pointless, all in vain. But he rises above the exhaustion and pain. He steels himself to his task. He becomes like a rock himself. He becomes harder than that rock.

I have hope. I have passion for my work. It's easy to steel myself and become like a rock. Many times my rock rolls back down the hill; sometimes it doesn't. If it rolls back down, I just start over again.

Jonathan:

Bob means don't get frustrated. Be prepared to wait forever for the project to get made. Just like when you are trying to sell the idea initially, don't take it personally. Don't let it get to you. Don't give up. While some projects move through development at a nice, brisk pace, most will not. Take the development process into account when you are negotiating your deal. Be as proactive and available as possible to ensure that your project keeps moving toward fruition. Of course, you should keep new and fresh projects flowing through the pipelines at all times.

Chapter 13

Sample High Concepts, Synopses, and Treatments

To give you a better idea of what we have been talking about, here are some sample high concepts, synopses, and treatments. Some are for projects, which are likely familiar. Some are for shows still in development as of this writing.

As we stated in Chapter 9, the biggest value of a treatment is the process of creating it. Treatments are colorful, dramatic, and convey the feel of a show or film. For the most part, we are the only people who will ever see our treatments. But without going through the pains of writing them, our projects would be incomplete. They would lack structure and character. We would miss some things we shouldn't, and our pitches would sound and feel less convincing.

We haven't included sample pitches here because pitches do not record well on paper. The voice, the gestures, and the overall enthusiasm are big parts of what makes a pitch successful.

GAME SHOWS

"Family Feud"

High concept
Teams of family members compete for cash.

Synopsis
A simple, trivia-for-the-Everyman game show in which two teams compete for cash. Every contestant and viewer will know at least one answer to each of our ultra-easy questions, which will be posed in a consistent format: "One hundred people surveyed, top answers on the board. The question is: What do school children eat for lunch?"

• *The hook:* Each team is comprised of five family members (i.e., the Smiths versus the Blakes). With its relative ease of questions and answers, multigenerational component, and high concept of one family team competing against another, "Family Feud" is a show that will appeal to the widest of demographics.

Treatment

Each team of five family members will be assembled into a panel, which will face its opposing team (stage left and stage right). The survey board will loom, above, upstage, center. The face-off podium with buzzers will be under the survey board.

The feud will be led and arbitrated by a comedic host, who will engage the competitors in interesting dialogue and playful banter.

Prior to the show, a random sampling of approximately 100 people will have been asked a variety of simple questions. Each round will feature a new question. All of the answers to that question will be up on the board, shielded from participant and audience view. Each answer's point value will depend on survey results.

When asked what school children eat for lunch, sixty-seven of the 100 people answered, "a peanut butter and jelly sandwich." The player who guesses this answer earns sixty-seven points. Twelve of the 100 people surveyed answered, "an apple," so a player who guesses "an apple" earns twelve points. For this particular question there are five more answers. However, the number of answers for each question will vary, depending on the survey results. "Places to go on a first date" might yield six answers, while there might be eight answers to the question "Animals you keep as a pet."

Each round begins when two players, one from each family (families must rotate team members for this), meet under the board and face-off to offer the speediest and most popular answer to a question. The face-off winner chooses (with help from the family) if his or her team will "pass" or "play."

The round continues. If choosing to "play," the team must correctly guess the remaining answers on the board. Each team member takes a turn, attempting to guess one of the remaining survey answers. Correct answers are awarded points. The round continues until all of the answers are revealed. However, if the team earns three "strikes," (makes three guesses that are not on the board), the opposing team may "steal" the round, including the first team's points, by guessing just one remaining answer correctly.

A new round begins. Rounds continue until either a team earns 300 points or time runs out. If time runs out, the team with the most points wins. The winning team moves to the next stage.

• *Next Stage:* "Fast Money" bonus round of survey questions for two members of the winning team (the family is free to choose who will play).

The first and second players are given fifteen and twenty seconds, respectively, to answer rapidly fired questions. When a player's answer matches an answer on the survey board, one point is awarded for each person in the survey who answered the same way (i.e.: The question is, "Reason to cancel a picnic." The player answers, "Rain." Eighty-three people in the survey answer, "Rain." The player receives eighty-three points). The first player takes a turn while the second waits in an offstage, soundproof area. Players may choose to pass on any number of questions. Player number two answers the same questions, but repeated answers (i.e., Rain) are rejected. If the team reaches 200 points, it is awarded $5,000. If less than 200 points accumulate, the team earns $5 per point.

After the show is established, we will periodically host a celebrity night, featuring cast members of popular sitcoms or soap operas, who will compete for charity. "Love Boat" versus "Three's Company" and "Eight is Enough" versus "Soap" will invigorate ratings and ensure one successful season after another.

"The Generation Game" (in development)
High concept
Pop culture trivia game in which two teams of three players (one player per team representing each of the 60s, 70s, and 80s generations) compete for a chance to win $1,000,000. Team success depends upon each member's knowledge of his or her own generation's pop culture.

Synopsis
A nostalgic trip down memory lane that the whole family can play, "The Generation Game" is the most complete pop culture trivia game show ever concocted. In addition to basic TV, music, politics, and movie categories for each generation, we include ad slogans, life-style trends, famous personalities, and other categories representative of specific generations. An articulate, well-dressed, well-informed host will read the questions and moderate the action.

Treatment

• *Round one:* "Seems Like Yesterday"

Six teams from the audience each send one representative to compete in a rapid-fire round of questions from the 1990s and 2000s. The random questions come from a wide variety of categories. Each has only one answer. There are no multiple choice, no true or false. Only the two highest scoring representatives qualify their teams for participation in the rest of the game.

• *Round two:* "On the Tube"

Players must answer questions derived from TV shows that aired in the decade (generation) they represent. Each member faces off against his generational counterpart on the other team for seven questions, or two minutes, whichever comes first. The first player to hit a buzzer gets a chance to answer the question. A player answering a question correctly is then tested with a true or false follow-up question.

The object is to run the board for as long as possible (up to the seven questions per category) without getting tripped up by the trick true or false follow-up question.

Although the team score is most important in the end, as individual generations face off, the player with the most individual points controls the board.

Example: 80s player on team A has 50 points, but the counterpart player on team B has 75 points; therefore, player B controls the subject when they face off and selects "TV Families."

Example question: What was the last name of the family on "Family Ties"?

Example follow-up, more specific question: Alex P. Keaton was a democrat. True or False?

Each correct answer is worth 25 points. Every correct follow-up answer is worth 10 points. A player maintains possession of the board until he answers incorrectly or is beaten to the buzzer by his counterpart. The counterpart must answer the question correctly to gain control of the board.

• *Round three:* "Personalities, Politics, and Potpourri"

In this round, general questions are pulled from the miscellanea of popular culture. Questions continue in the same manner, but correct answers earn 30 points and 30 points are deducted for incorrect answers.

• *Round four:* "On the Radio"

Questions about popular music comprise this round. Each correct answer is worth 40 points. Each incorrect answer loses 40 points. Surprise bonus questions following a correct answer are randomly sprinkled throughout this round. These bonus questions are worth 100 points for a correct answer and a minus 100 points for an incorrect answer.

Example: The 70s player on Team B has more points than his counterpart on Team A and selects "One Hit Wonders." He answers the question correctly and earns 40 points. A random bonus question appears and, since he was the last contestant with a correct answer, he gets a shot at it. He answers correctly and adds 100 points to his score. There is no penalty for passing on the bonus questions, but an incorrect answer would have cost the contestant 100 points.

• *Round five:* "On the Big Screen"

The player with the *least points* controls the game to start this round, but he may only select questions from his own generation. A correct answer is worth 50 points. An incorrect answer loses 50 points. In this round, each player may apply a "block" one time to prevent a point loss or to prevent the other player from stealing control of the board. Blocks may be utilize one time per player.

• *Round six:* "Crossing the Generations—Free for All"

The team with the least amount of points controls the board and selects a category from any of the three generations. The first team to buzz with the correct answer takes control of the board and may then pick a question from any generation. Points that may be gained or lost remain at 50.

• *Championship round:* The winning team elects one of their players to try to answer as many questions as possible in the span of 75 seconds. The questions are from the chosen player's generation, but the category is randomly selected. Each correct answer is worth $5,000. Two passes and two wrong answers are permitted before elimination. Twelve correct answers in the 75 seconds earns $1,000,000 for the team!

Reality Shows

"Extreme Makeover"

High concept

Less than perfect folks from across the country leave home for six weeks and receive multiple plastic surgeries, which yield astounding results.

Synopsis

It's the Cinderella story, reality-style. Each week we watch two individuals become new people as they leave their friends and family, undergo several plastic surgery procedures, repair and whiten teeth, cut or add hair, shop for a new wardrobe, and shed pounds. When these transformed subjects return to their home towns for the big "reveal" parties, even lifelong friends will hardly recognize them!

Treatment

After a nationwide search, producing thousands of written applications, the most needy and interesting candidates will be invited to participate in this destiny-altering opportunity. Viewers will watch as our "Extreme Team" of top plastic surgeons, cosmetic dentists, hair and makeup artists, and personal trainers change lives.

Each hour-long episode will be self-contained and will feature two extreme makeovers. Possible makeover candidates include (but are not limited to) people who are suffering from the effects of profound weight loss, are the less-attractive half of twins, are accident or burn victims, and folks who just plain hate the way they look. Candidates' stories, personalities, and needs will differ greatly from one another.

Both stories run concurrently. Little by little we watch each participant transform, saving the big pay-off (the reveal party) for the last ten minutes of the show.

Format

• *First segment:* "The Before"

Introduction to each of the candidates. We meet spouses, children, friends, parents, teachers, and bosses, gathering background stories and building empathy.

• *Second and subsequent segments:* "The Ex-treme Makeover"

We watch each and every step of the journey as the candidates move toward their new lives. We are in the operating rooms, dentist offices, workout clubs, salons, and shops.

Family and friends back home are interviewed. We feel their nervous anticipation, fears, and excitement.

Viewers learn new eating habits, new exercise re-gimes, hair and makeup tips as we watch the candi-dates heal, become more healthy, and transform!

• *Final segment:* "The Reveal Party"

The two positively shocking payoffs are reserved for the last few minutes and keep viewers glued to the TV for the entire hour-long episode. Now, happier and healthier people, the former candidates are reintro-duced into their respective worlds. Each is the guest of honor at his or her reveal-night party, arriving fashion-ably late in a limo and dressed in formal attire. Friends and family scream, laugh, and produce tears of joy at the first sight of this exhilarated and more confident loved one.

"Revenge, Inc." (in development)

High concept

"Punked" with a purpose: "Cops" meets "Cheat-ers" meets "Candid Camera."

Synopsis

Simple, low-budget shows like "Cheaters" and "Cops" have enjoyed both domestic and international success for years. They provide for a slow, steady burn and have garnered a worldwide, cult-like following. Here's the next generation, which adds sharp wit and humor to the usual "train wreck TV" formula: Our cre-ative team of Fab Five-style comedians (think: "Queer Eye For the Straight Guy") designs and stages out-landish acts of revenge upon the folks who deserve it the most. The demographics are wide, gathering view-ers from three distinct groups: the Jerry Springer set, "TV's Bloopers and Practical Jokes" crowd, and those brilliant folks who appreciate wry, edgy, extreme hu-mor. "Revenge, Inc." will be comprised of one or two 20-minute, 3-part segments, can be regionally pro-duced on a shoestring budget.

Treatment

These folks need to be taught a lesson: the bully from high school; the overbearing boss; the ex-lover, who did you wrong; the loud, obnoxious neighbors; that tow-truck company bounty hunter, who wrongly towed your car; the inconsiderate, messy, or late-paying-the-bills roommate; the former friend, who stole your money, lover, or job. The list (and we all have one) is neverending!

Format

• *Part one:* The creative team sifts through faxes and e-mails and selects a worthy "complainant." We meet the complainant and learn the horrific background story through footage and interviews. Filled with compassion, viewers are ready to see the bad guy (or girl) pay!

• *Part two:* The comedians devise and setup the revenge scenario, working with the complainant for maximum impact. The practical joke punishment is brilliant and must always fit the crime.

• *Part three:* The ambush-style revenge scene...the big payoff!

• *Final one or two minutes of the show:* A follow-up interview with this week's bad guy and/or updates of complainants and bad guys from previous shows, providing the viewer with closure and establishing a through-line.

• *Credit rollover:* One of our comedians makes a crank call to someone who has done *him* wrong.

REALITY-GAME SHOW HYBRID

"American Idol"

High concept

The search for America's next superstar.

Synopsis

In search of the next great singing sensation, this show opens the floodgates of undiscovered talent from across the nation. We are front row and center for it all: from the worst auditions ever captured on tape to astonishing performances of world-class caliber. Three expert judges offer criticism, suggestions, and selections. Ultimately, America decides who will prevail, as one contestant is eliminated each week—leaving one "Idol" with a record deal and a hungry group of fans, awaiting his or her first release.

Treatment

• In the preliminary episodes, we travel to the regional rounds of auditions.

•*Prescreening:* After prescreening thousands of singers on location (Los Angeles, Detroit, Atlanta, Miami, New York City, Nashville, and Austin), the "American Idol" staff will have chosen "recalls" for the first televised round of auditions.

Recall selection will have been based on talent, ability, look, and style. Some will be fabulous; some will be horrible.

• *The first round:* Here is our point of entry. In these first episodes, viewers will alternately marvel and wince at the recalled contestants' varying ability levels. Our entertaining panel of expert judges (Paula Abdul, attached) will give accolades, impart advice, and choose who will continue to the second audition in Hollywood.

• *Next episodes*—Second auditions in Los Angeles. Contestants from across the country will sing their hearts out, in hopes of landing one of the thirty finalist slots. The panel members are refreshingly—and often painfully—candid as they make selections for the real competition still to come. These finalists must commit to staying in Los Angeles for the duration of the show.

• *Bulk of the season*—Final auditions (in stages). Our thirty finalists will be separated into three groups of ten.

• *Week One:* The first group of ten competes against each other, over a period of four nights. At the week's end, America decides which three will advance to the next stage.

• *Week Two:* The second group competes; three advance.

• *Week Three:* The third group competes; three advance. These three weeks yield nine ultra-talented singers. All the while, the panel continues to reprimand, correct, and encourage. They will choose a wild card from the left-behind twenty-one, leaving a total of ten competitors who will move to the next stage. These three weeks will have reality elements (ala MTV's "The Real World"), allowing viewers to become attached to their favorites.

Our remaining ten finalists showcase their talents two to four nights per week, over a period of several weeks. This is astronaut training for singers! Each must stretch his or her voice to compete in the musical theme of the night (i.e., Elton John, Aretha Franklin, etc.), as America slowly shrinks the finalist group from ten to one.

Only one will become the next "American Idol."

"Courting Anna" (in development)

High concept

Regular guys compete against each other *and* Anna Kournikova to earn her respect, attention, and— ultimately— a weekend with her, which will be the envy of every red-blooded male in the universe.

Synopsis

Join Anna Kournikova as she challenges ten suitors to a series of extreme physical and mental challenges. These romance warriors must compete against each other and against *Anna!* The winner gets Anna all to himself on a fantasy date, the likes of which only the wealthiest and most elite have experienced. "Anna Boot Camp," "Anna Fear Factor," and an exhausting menu of other "Anna Challenges" will separate the men from the boys and finally give Anna the chance to meet her match.

Treatment

What if the most beautiful woman in the world could kick your ass? What if she were braver than you? Had a better memory than you? What if she could eat more than you or were more clever than you? What if she could do almost everything better than you? If you don't think it's possible, than you don't know Russian superstar, Anna Kournikova.

Forget for a moment what you think you know about Anna. Forget that she is universally recognized as the sexiest woman on Earth. Forget she is responsible for single handily changing the face of women's sports forever. And forget she is the intoxicating beauty who flashes her million-dollar smile for grateful sponsors, drives men all over the world wild, and that has inspired an entire generation of woman. Forget all of that for a moment and discover what is really unique about this amazing superstar.

Anna Kournikova is an intelligent, wild, and fearless beauty with an unparalleled appetite for everything that life offers. She exudes confidence, determination, and passion to succeed on every level. She is brash, brazen, and bold in ways usually reserved for cartoon superheroes. She's humble, well spoken, and thoughtful. She's a tomboy. She's demanding. She's extreme. She's funny. She's playful. She's wealthy. She's 22. Anna Kournikova seems to have it all, but she does lack one thing—a man that can keep up with her.

• *Episode one:* Men from all over the country have sent videotapes, demonstrating just how far they are willing to go in order to win Anna's attention: getting tattooed, shaving their bodies, singing and dancing, scaling buildings, and jumping off cliffs. We'll get a taste of the most extreme and outlandish acts that Anna's fans will do to prove their devotion. The gloves are off, as her most faithful fans (some hot, some not) go the distance for the woman of their dreams.

Accompanied by her mother and best friend, Anna will view the video submissions and will react from her gut. From amusement and intrigue to total disgust, she will share her opinions, as she whittles down the candidates to her ten favorites (and a few runner-ups, for last minute "bad behavior" substitutions).

The runner-ups will be on-call in the "Anna Van," which will standby with the eager replacements, ready to jump in should one of the original ten be eliminated. Throughout the show, we will cut to the alternates in the Anna van to get their reactions to the competition.

• *Episode two:* Anna's top ten suitors begin the battle to win her favor. This episode will feature one physical challenge and one field pageant event (talent, bathing suit, etc.). There are no scheduled eliminations, but Anna may choose to send someone packing at any point during the first three episodes.

This episode is set at the beach where our competitors will have to, say, pull themselves into a moving helicopter from a speedboat. The stunts will vary, but all will be demanding and visually impressive.

After proving their physical prowess, our ten must strut their stuff in bathing suits, in an effort to show that they've got the looks to back up their brawn.

• *Episode three:* The next physical challenge and field pageant are set at a dude ranch, where our competitors must battle a bull, break a wild pony, locate a tennis ball in a manure-filled pigsty, or milk a cow…sans hands!

After getting down and dirty, it is time for the talent show. Anna is still free to reject any of her suitors at any point—and that's just what the alternates in the Anna Van are praying will happen.

• *Episode four:* The final physical challenge and field pageant combination is set in the snow-covered mountains of Aspen. After one last icy daredevil challenge, we'll see how the guys stack up in an interview situation.

Sitting by the fire in the luxurious lodge, they must answer Anna's most provocative questions. After careful deliberation, Anna will make her final selection, choosing one of her suitors to be crowned…or not?

Just as Anna's "regular Joe" hero thinks he's got it made, she takes the wind out his sails. Though he has truimphed over his comrades, he is informed that he has actually only won half the battle.

The twist: The *real* competition for Anna will now begin as our hero meets his match in…a billionaire, a celebrity, *and a royal!*

Let the real games begin!

• *Episodes five, six, and seven:* The final four take group outings, and the stakes have never been higher. We will now see how our "hero" fares against his new opponents. Can he take the heat? How will the fabulous new competitors deal with their lowly competition? Who will dazzle with wit, charm, and intellect? Who will impress her with physical prowess? "Courting Anna" enters the realm of "Lifestyles of the Rich and Famous," and the competition heats up. Our bachelors try to one-up each other in an extreme battle of brains, brawn, and bling bling!

• *Episode eight* (two-hour special): One by one, our four suitors will be summoned to a special "Anna Suite" at a fabulous resort, where they are all now staying. Via speakerphone, Anna selects the lucky man of the day and tells him what she is in the mood to do. Each contestant will only have one hour to pull out all the stops and furiously plan his only moments alone with the object of his desire. But as her time is precious, these extreme dates must be brief. After each contender has taken his final and best shot at courting Anna, we tease the dramatic concluding episode, in which the winner will be crowned.

• *Episode nine:* After weeks of angst for our four bachelors, the ball is in Anna's court. She will address each of them and point out his strengths and weaknesses, as we take a look back at his journey. Finally, Anna will make her choice.

After bidding the three losers farewell, Anna and the winner will embark on a fantasy vacation to places exotic, elite, and expensive. With the world's most beautiful and brave woman on his arm, this is a dream come true. Victory has never been so sweet.

MOVIES

Mrs. Doubtfire

High Concept

Divorced dad is denied visitation with his kids, so he puts on a dress and takes a job as their nanny.

Synopsis

An extremely high concept comedy about a flawed father who is *desperate* to stay close to his kids in the wake of a recent divorce. Having exhausted all other options, he decides to dress, speak, and act like a sweet, middle-aged English woman and apply for a job as a nanny...to his own kids!

While his ex-wife has moved on with her life and found a serious, more successful love interest, our hero is forced to undertake a painful game of dual identity. In the process he learns the truth about his kids and himself. In the end, his newfound perspective brings his family back into a functioning unit...happily ever-after. It is a modern-day spin on the classic film, *Mary Poppins*, with comedic cross-dressing elements from *Tootsie*.

Treatment

A husband and father of three children, Daniel

Hillard is an eccentric actor and a talented voice-over artist. When he leaves his latest cartoon gig (for reasons of conscience) and throws a forbidden petting zoo birthday party for his son, his wife, Miranda, has had enough. After the couple locks into a stormy argument (she is sick-to-death of looking like "the bad guy"), Miranda asks for a divorce. She is a successful architect and designer, a serious and organized woman. In addition to their clear personality differences, she admits to her husband that she no longer loves him. Daniel is taken aback. He does not want this. He loves his wife and family. Miranda holds firm.

At Uncle Frank and Aunt Jack's (they are life partners and make-up artists), Daniel spins his tale of woe. He is heart-sick but assures them that Miranda will change her mind.

• *Cut to:* The divorce proceedings, where the judge explains that the temporary custody arrangement allows Daniel only one day per week with his children. The matter will be revisited in 90 days. Within those 90 days, Daniel must secure a dwelling and employment.

As Dad moves out, the children grieve. End of Act One.

He meets with his stern court-liaison who reiterates the judge's requirements for granting a more liberal visitation schedule. Daniel explains he is an actor. He tries out a myriad of voices and improv bits, but she'll have none of it. His new job will be boxing and shipping film cans and equipment for a local TV station. Though it's miserable work, he is glad to have found it for the sake of his kids.

Back at Miranda's job, she meets with Stuart—her handsome, successful, former boyfriend—about a future project. Sparks fly.

On Saturday, the kids visit Dad's small, yet-to-be unpacked, dingy apartment. Over dinner, the children pepper him with questions about the divorce. He becomes frustrated and angry. The meal ends when Mom shows up an hour early for pickup and criticizes his shabby living conditions. The ex-spouses argue bitterly, and the children are distraught. We learn that she is placing an ad for a nanny. Dad will happily do the job for free, but Mom resists. When her back is turned, Daniel changes the contact numbers on her ad application, so no one will be able to respond.

He employs his acting skills and harangues her with "responses" to her ad. All of his characters would be terrible nannies! His plan is working, and Miranda becomes desperate just as the last phone call is placed. Daniel's "Mrs. Doubtfire" is the perfect nanny, a breath of fresh air. An interview is arranged.

• *Montage:* Uncle Frank and Aunt Jack try out dozens of wigs and costumes, make-up styles, and accessories while Daniel works on voice possibilities. They decide to go over the top with a latex mask and fat suit. "Mrs. Doubtfire" is born!

At the family home, the interview goes beautifully. Miranda and Mrs. Doubtfire share a cup of tea. As the conversation rolls around to the topic of the divorce, Daniel realizes that he will be privy to Miranda's inner-thoughts. This could be a boon on many levels.

On the way home his stockings fall, exposing his hairy legs. His back hurts, and the bus driver flirts with him. Exhausted, he finally reaches his apartment, only to meet the stern court-liaison. He'd forgotten about the home visits and now must pretend to be his own older sister.

Antics ensue. He changes in and out of his complicated costume, trying in vain to play both characters. In the chaos his latex mask falls out of the window and is run over by a fire truck. To cover, he plunges his face into a cake. Chunks of frosting plunge into the liaison's tea; she grows suspicious. End of Act Two.

Uncle Jack makes another mask. We watch Daniel's two lives: punching the clock at the TV station and being the perfect nanny. Mrs. Doubtfire runs a tight ship. The children must do homework, clean house, and never talk back. As the nanny, Daniel must learn to provide order, healthy meals, and consistency.

• *Montage:* After the obligatory kitchen disaster scene (he catches the breast of his fat suit on fire), he watches cooking shows and takes notes. He learns to prepare lobster. Mrs. Doubtfire rides bikes with the children and reads to the youngest daughter.

All is working well until the ex-boyfriend, Stuart, enters the home. Mrs. Doubtfire explains to Miranda that it's too early to date and that she should probably never date—for the sake of the kids. Later, Daniel's son walks in on Mrs. Doubtfire using the restroom…standing up! Dad confesses the scheme to the two oldest kids, but it must remain their little secret if he is to keep the nanny job.

In another heart-to-heart talk, Miranda tells Mrs. Doubtfire that the court-liaison found an older, unattractive woman in Daniel's apartment pretending to be his sister. The conversation turns back to the divorce and the subject of Daniel. Miranda reveals all of her feelings to her nanny, the good and bad. Ironically, this is the only cohesive, productive conversation we see between Mom and Dad, and it is bitter-sweet.

Mrs. Doubtfire brings the family to meet Stuart at his posh country club pool. From the tiki bar, "she" watches in pain as this interloper moves in on the family.

Daniel is back at the TV station, playing with toy dinosaurs on a set. The dinosaurs rap about their demise and their current state: crude oil. His main character is a cooler, hipper Mr. Rogers. The station's general manager watches from the shadows and is impressed. He invites Daniel to a dinner meeting Monday evening at a restaurant named Bridges to discuss show ideas. Daniel is dazzled by such an opportunity!

On Saturday, Miranda arrives at Daniel's *bright and clean* apartment. She is impressed to find the children eating a home-cooked meal. Daniel explains that he has learned how to cook, sew, and clean house. He asks once again to be the children's nanny. Miranda says that she could never fire Mrs. Doubtfire. She is too wonderful; the children love her.

Days later, Miranda and the kids relentlessly plead with Mrs. Doubtfire to please come to Miranda's birthday dinner, which Stuart is hosting—also on Monday at Bridges! "She" vigorously resists but is compelled to agree in the end. End of Act Three.

More antics in the farcical climatic scene: At Bridges, Daniel must change out and in and out of his costume, juggling the table with his prospective new boss and the table with his family and Stuart. Once again he tries in vain to play both characters. He drinks too much at the dinner meeting and loses his fake teeth at the birthday dinner. He sneaks into the kitchen and adds cayenne pepper to Stuart's meal. Back at the dinner meeting, the general manager wonders why Daniel is wearing perfume and lipstick. It all becomes too much, and Daniel accidentally returns to the dinner meeting as Mrs. Doubtfire! He covers: This is his idea for a TV show. Suddenly, Stuart begins to violently choke on a shrimp. Mrs. Doubtfire rushes back to the birthday dinner and heroically performs the Heimlich maneuver, but he loses part of the latex mask in the process. A shocked, flustered, and furious Miranda storms out of Bridges, taking the children with her. End of Act Four.

In court, Dad defends his actions. He loves his kids and was willing to do anything to be with them. They are his life. He needs them. Miranda seems touched but remains silent. The unsympathetic judge awards full custody to Miranda and grants Daniel *court-supervised* visitations.

Mom is interviewing new nannies, and the search is not going well. All miss Mrs. Doubtfire (even Mom), but she explains that Mrs. Doubtfire wasn't a real person. They must move on. Just then, Mrs. Doubtfire's voice can be heard from the living room TV. The family gathers around to watch Daniel's comfy and smart TV show, starring Mrs. Doubtfire.

Days later, Miranda visits Daniel on the show's set. She explains that Mrs. Doubtfire brought out the best in all of them and they all miss her.

Back at the house, the kids watch their dad's show. The doorbell rings. It's Daniel. Miranda has taken care of the court issue and Dad will now be watching them after school each day. The kids are thrilled! The family will heal.

Jolly Roger (in development)

High concept

Computer Age pirate loots from the rich and gives to the poor, using high-tech plundering methods.

Synopsis

Roger made his billions in the tech boom and is now a reluctant man of leisure. He throws splashy parties, hosts charity functions, and is quite a ladies' man. But Roger derives no joy from this wealthy life-style of the idle rich and longs for something more. He and techie friends take to the high seas and become modern-day, Computer Age pirates.

Treatment

Immediately upon making new acquaintances, Roger rushes them off to his hobby wing. In these rooms, he displays his prized possessions: Pirate paraphernalia! Pirate antiques! Pirate memorabilia! Pirate weaponry! Shelves of dusty books on pirates! He is not insane. Roger has had a lifelong fascination with pirates, and now he has the money to heavily invest in his collection. But even his extensive collection can't provide this brilliant, active man with the stimulation he requires.

He assembles a group of favorite former employees. This is a colorful, uber-brainy crew of "Merry Men." Together, these minds can move mountains! A new form of charitable organization is established. End of Act One.

The team invents and schemes and hacks and creates. Within weeks, Roger is on the high seas! His ship is decked-out in literally unheard of, high tech decadence. The crew mans gadgets, screens and dishes. This stuff makes James Bond look like a character on the "Flintstones." Enabled to stealthily plunder riches from drug smugglers, evil business empires, etc., Roger is living out his boyhood dream! He freely gives all of his loot to various charities, and no one is ever physically harmed.

After several months, Roger and crew are world famous. Hollywood, the media, and big business all cash in on his adventures. Everyone knows what he's doing, and no one wants to stop him. Charities love him. He has developed a cult-like following with the public. Women worship him. Since he's never hurt anyone and he only robs evildoers, the law stays out of it—besides, he's never been caught in the act. Jolly Roger is exactly what the world needs.

But the drug smugglers are less than thrilled. So are many corporations. They are losing revenue and tired of the terrible PR. These two groups come together to defeat this modern-day swashbuckler, and Roger ends up in jail.

While awaiting trial, he is as good spirited as a prisoner can be. To him, it's better than being bored in his lonely mansion. Fellow inmates and guards love him.

There is a public outcry! Protests! Sit-ins! Marches! Free Jolly Roger! But even his dream team of lawyers can't get him off the hook. Roger is found guilty and will have to serve twenty-five years to life! End of Act Two.

Right on cue, his crew launches a massive escape attempt. They've invented and hacked and created unbelievable tools for the job! This is an escape like no other: innovative, flashy, and funny. Roger even frees a few wrongly convicted inmates on the way out.

One month later, they are all back at work on the high seas. They've kept the escape gadgets, as they may come in handy for their next big adventure. End of Act Three.

Some notes

The character of Roger could be cast as a woman (think: Laura Croft).

This simple, action-adventure story works on many levels, examining the true meaning of right versus wrong.

Fine-tuning could make the film appropriate for younger audiences or gear it toward the more adult, James Bond crowd.

The story's end is wide open, perfect for a sequel.

Jolly Roger merchandising is a no-brainer, especially if the film is geared toward kids and teens.

Glossary of Terms

- **Adaptation:** story that has been already written in another form (book, play, short story, etc.

- **Agent:** a broker of talent and/or properties who works on commission (generally 10%)

- **Antagonist:** may or may not be the "villain" in the story, but will always oppose the protagonist

- **Arc:** the rising and falling structure of the story

- **Assistant:** the right hand for producers and execs…also the keeper of the gate

- **Attach (-ed) (-ment):** stars or directors who are interested in the project—said be be "attached". Usually a positive. If too much talent is attached, the project is said to have *baggage*

- **Back-end Deal:** paid after the project has been produced and has made money

- **Bible:** an extensive, formal treatment for a TV series

- **Bidding War:** occurs when two or more buyers want the same property

- **Buzz:** the word on the street, the grapevine, the rumor mill ... all positive

- **Castability:** project carries appeal for A-list talent

- **Commercial Viability:** marketability. Will project sell, get produced, and will it find a viewership?

- **Concept:** an idea

- **Conflict:** varying degrees of tension that drive the plot and create interest

- **Copyright:** legal protection of property

- **Coverage:** the paperwork generated by readers who evaluate scripts; includes a synopsis and evaluation

- **Deal:** the project is moving forward

- **Deferred:** paid on the backend

- **Demographic:** defines a specific audience

- **Development:** time period in the life of a project: after the purchase, before production. Story is reworked, parts are cast, script is rewritten. May last several years

- **Development Girl (or Boy):** unusually young and hip production office employee who researches cultural trends through social events, buzz, and the like. Ranks above an assistant and below a junior exec

- **Dollar Option:** after paying one dollar, buyer controls property for a set period of time

- **Entertainment Property:** an idea, a script, a film, a show. It can be bought and sold like any other good or service

- **Exec:** short for executive. Refers to a higher-up in a studio. In many cases— the buyer

- **Executive Producer:** TV: creator and/ or writer of show. FILM: the deal—making producer

- **Greenlight:** the "go ahead" for a project

- **High Concept:** the meat of the pitch, summed up in one or two sentences

- **Hook:** an attention grabbing incident, twist, or detail

- **Leave-behind:** treatment, synopsis, or visual aid that is left for potential buyer

- **Legs:** an idea is said to have legs if it needs minimal pitching. It can travel and stand on its own, without lengthy description

- **Logline:** a sentence or phrase that gives the flavor of an idea and creates interest for it

- **Meeting:** a scheduled pitch session with a potential buyer

- **Merchandizing:** products that materialize from a project. Asking for a portion of the merchandizing can be a good idea. Consider: *Toy Story*

- **Option:** acquiring control over a property (verb) or the term for the legal document by which the producer acquires control (noun)

- **Packaging:** attaching the talent (actors, director, writer, etc.), making the project more desirable

- **Pitch:** to enthusiastically explain a project to a potential buyer (verb); can also be used as a noun

- **Pitchman (or woman):** in the industry, one who sells entertainment properties

- **Physical Production:** production side that includes line production, unit production managing, production coordination, and production assisting. The role-up-your-sleeves and/or use a calculator end of production

- **Player:** one who regularly makes high-profile deals in the industry

- **Plot:** the storyline, comprised of conflict and a beginning, middle, and end

- **Plot Twist:** an unexpected turn of events in the story

- **Post-production:** portion of a project's life, which follows shooting: editing, additional dialogue recording, sound effects, music, etc.

- **Premise:** theme, focus, or moral of story

- **Pre-production:** the tail end of development: shooting locations secured, crew assembled, last minute casting, director works through script, etc.

- **Producer Credit:** listed as an associate producer, co-producer, producer, exec producer

- **Production Company:** company that produces TV shows or movies. May be under the control of a large studio or exist independently

- **Property:** the material upon which a TV show or movie is based (script, play, treatment, book, etc.), a treatment, synopsis, or registered idea

- **Protagonist:** the lead character in the story. Can be a hero, anti-hero, or even a villain. Audience sympathizes with him

- **Public Domain:** term that describes the state of a property which is not protected under copyright laws

- **Reader:** in the industry, one who reads scripts and provides coverage for producers and execs

- **Release Form:** see "Studio Release Agreement"

- **Rights:** ownership or temporary control of a property

- **Samuel French Bookstores:** in L.A., N.Y., and Toronto. Stores carry scripts, plays, the trades, contact information, reference information. An invaluable resource for writrers!

- **Screenplay:** script for a movie

- **Setting:** time, place, and general atmosphere of a story

- **Spec (on spec):** short for speculation; work done without a contract

- **Stock Scenes**: highly visual scenes with which we are all familiar: car chases, explosions, etc.

- **Story Bonus:** a pre-negotiated payment made once a project is completed

- **Studios:** Disney, Universal, Paramount, Fox, Warner Brothers, and many more. These large corporations are able to buy or generate properties from within, produce them, as well as distribute and promote them

- **Studio Release Agreement:** a legally binding document, stating that if the studio hears your idea/ or reads your script, you will not sue them for plagarizing

- **Subplot:** less obvious storyline, which re-enforces the main plot

- **Synopsis:** a short and to-the-point summary of the plot. Very useful when formulating a pitch

- **Talent:** actors and directors

- **Tag:** an interesting characteristic or repetitive gesture, which will make a character more memorable

- **Three-Act Structure:** The beginning, middle, and end of a story, treatment or movie. Five-act structures and also used

- ***Thomas Guide:*** guidebook of L.A. freeways and streets

- **Trades:** *Variety* and *The Hollywood Reporter*. Magazines that chronicle the business of show business

- **Treatment:** a longer, more dramatic telling of the story than the synopsis

- **Turnaround:** the process of reselling a project

- **Vehicle:** project which could provide breakthrough roles for talent

- **Viewpoint:** the character through whom the story is told

- **W.G.A. (Writers' Guild of America):** professional association that helps and protects writers of television, film, and radio. Offices are in New York and Los Angeles

References & Resources

Academy of Motion Picture Arts & Sciences
(Provides film screenings, events, entertainment news.)

8949 Wilshire Blvd.

Beverly Hills, CA 90211

www.oscars.com

310-247-3000

Academy of Television Arts & Sciences
(Hosts educational events for the public, internships, and valuable networking opportunities.)

5220 Lankershim Blvd., 2nd Floor

North Hollywood, CA 91601

www.emmys.tv

818-754-2800

American Society of Composers, Authors & Publishers—L.A.
(Source for entertainment news, hosts workshops, assists in career development.)

7920 Sunset Blvd,. Ste. 300

Los Angeles, CA 90046

www.ascap.com

323-883-1000

Cynthia's Cynopsis
(Free subscription, daily online newsletter; provides up-to-date TV ratings and rankings, industry news, job listings, fun TV facts.)

www.cynopsis.com

Hollywood Creative Directory
(Reference book—new additions three times a year; provides up-to-date industry contact information to subscribers, film-maker resources.)

www.hcdonline.com

The Hollywood Reporter
(Industry "trade" paper; information on business side of the industry; lists projects in production; announces mergers, exec promotions, casting news, etc.; reviews; also an excellent free online version available.)

www.hollywoodreporter.com

Hot Docs: Canadian International Documentary Festival
(Provides a terrific pitch workshop and offers project funding opportunities for documentary films.)

517 College St., Ste. 420

Toronto, Ontario, Canada M6G 4A2

www.hotdocs.ca

1-416-203-2155

IDFA: Internation Documentary Film Festival Amsterdam

(Provides pitching opportunities to stimulate coproduction and cofinancing of documentary film projects.)

Kleine-Gartmanplantsoen 10

1017 RR Amsterdam

The Netherlands

www.theforum.nl

+31 20 627 3329

Motion Picture Association of America

(Great site to research viewer demographics.)

15503 Ventura Blvd.

Encino, CA 91436

www.mpaa.org

818-995-6600

Producers' 411

(Reference book—updated once a year; gives contact info for studios, networks, and nearly every independent production company; provides filmmaker resources; user-friendly website gives partial access to both N.Y. and L.A. versions.)

www.411publishing.com

323-965-2020

Producers Guild of America

(Provides everything from free film screenings to health insurance: valuable resource for both beginning and veteran producers.)

8530 Wilshire Blvd., Ste 450

Beverly Hills, CA 90211

www.producersguild.org

310-358-9020

Samuel French Bookstore
(Sells screenplays of produced films, books on filmmaking and screenwriting; provides entertainment industry resource guides.)

7623 Sunset Blvd.
Hollywood, CA 90046
www.samuelfrench.com
323-876-0570

New York Office:
45 W.25th St.
New York, NY 10010
www.samuelfrench.com
212-206-8990

Toronto Office:
100 Lombard St.
Toronto, ON, Canada M5C 1M3
www.samuelfrench.com
416-363-3536

Sundance Institute
(Hosts workshops and conferences for writing, directing, producing, and acting; also provides volunteer opportunities for Sundance Film Festival.)

8857 W. Olympic Blvd.
Beverly Hills, CA 90211
www.sundance.org
310-360-1981

United States Copyright Office
(Register property, learn about your rights and protections.)

Library of Congress
Washington D.C. 20559

www.loc.gov/copyright
202-707-3000

Women in Film

(Provides education, funding, screenings, and support for women in the industry.)

P.O. Box 17706

Encino, CA 91416

www.wif.org

310-657-5144

Writers Guild of America—East

(Provides legal support, entertainment news, free screenings and industry discussion panels, research assistance, registration services, and inspiration.)

555 W. 57th St., Ste. 1230

New York, NY 10019

www.wgaeast.org

212-767-7800

Writers Guild of America—West

7000 W. Third St.

Los Angeles, CA 90048

www.wga.org

323-951-4000

Writers Guild of Canada

123 Edward St., Ste. 1225

Toronto, ON M5G 1E2 Canada

www.writersguildofcanada.com

800-567-9974

Variety
(Industry "trade" paper; info on business side of the industry; lists projects in production; announces mergers, exec promotions, etc.—daily and weekly versions available, also an online version.)

5700 Wilshire Blvd., Ste. 120
Los Angeles, CA 90036
323-857-6600
www.variety.com

ADDITIONAL READING

- *Adventures in the Screen Trade* by William Goldman

- *All You Need to Know About the Movie and TV Business* by Gail Resnik

- *The Art of Adaptation* by Linda Seger

- *The Complete Encyclopedia of Television Programs: 1947–1979* by Terrence Vincent

- *Fade In: The Screenwriting Process* by Robert A. Berman

- *Getting Your Script Through the Hollywood Maze* by Linda Stuart

- *Hello, He Lied, and Other Truths from the Hollywood Trenches* by Lynda Obst

- *How to Write a Movie in 21 Days* by Vicki King

- *The Journal*—monthly publication by the Writers Guild of America—West

- *Selling a Screenplay* by Sid Field

- *Television Writing from Concept to Contract* by Richard A. Blum

- *The TV Scriptwriter's Handbook* by Alfred Brenner

- *The Screenwriter's Problem Solver* by Syd Fields

- *Steal This Plot: A Writer's Guide to Story, Structure, and Plagiarism* by June and William Noble

- *Writer's Guide to Hollywood Producers, Directors, and Screenwriter's Agents—* Skip Press

- *The Writer's Legal Guide* by Tad Crawford and Tony Lyons

- *A Writer's Time* by Kenneth Atchity.

- *Writing Treatments That Sell* by Kenneth Atchity and Chi-Li Wong

- *Unsold Television Plots* by Lee Goldberg

Index

For free reports on writing and getting
published, visit QuillDriverBooks.com

About the Authors

Jonathan Koch is under a producing deal at Asylum Entertainment based at 20th Century Fox in Los Angeles. Asylum is in its fifth year of producing the Emmy-nominated series "Beyond the Glory" for Fox. Among his various network and studio producing deals, Koch has recently created, sold, and will executive produce "Courting Anna" a reality series featuring Anna Kournikova, "Worst Day of Your Life," and "The Assistant." He also created and sold the game show "American Hold 'Em" to the Walt Disney Company. Koch and partner, Steve Michaels, are currently under contract to produce the feature "Murderer's Row" for HBO. Michaels and Koch are also negotiating studio deals on "The Inventor" starring George Foreman, and the reality soap "Love Is in the Heir."

Prior to serving as creator and executive producer of MTV's reality pilot "Tranced," Koch completed his obligations under contract at Merv Griffin Entertainment where, in addition to his executive producing responsibilities, Koch served as an executive for the company. Among the various feature and television projects developed under the Griffin Entertainment banner, Koch created and developed the "Face-Off" game show which was sold to Twentieth Television, as well as "Good Samaritan" which was sold to The Walt Disney Company. Koch also served as executive producer on the pilot entitled "The Court of Common Sense" starring "Fear Factor" host Joe Rogan. In addition, Koch has cocreated and will serve as executive producer on a new game show for CBS entitled "Generation Game" which is in active development.

Prior to joining the Griffin Group, Koch was founder, president, and CEO of Gravy Train Productions, a marketing, licensing, and promotional company specializing in the development and implementation of entertainment-based programs and events.

The core focus of the company is the exploitation of branded entertainment properties within both the content community and the traditional commerce sector. Since its inception in 1993, Gravy Train Productions' entrepreneurial focus has expanded to include talent representation, packaging, project development, contract negotiations, ancillary endorsement opportunities, and worldwide personal promotional appearances.

Gravy Train has successfully created and produced over 150 promotional events for corporate clients including General Mills, Microsoft, Edelman Public Relations, FAO Schwarz, Kentucky Fried Chicken, Kellogg's, Tribune Broadcasting, Six Flags, Sports Car Racing and many others. In 1998, Gravy Train Productions partnered with the Hasbro team to promote and market the launch of "Pokemon" in the United States.

Koch is also President and CEO of Dawg Pound Productions, Inc. Since 1997, Dawg Pound Productions has served as the packaging/production entity for the assets of Gravy Train Productions. Dawg Pound Productions has developed and executive produced numerous television projects including three telefilms for NBC.

In November of 1996, Koch was one of two founding partners in Celebrity Sightings, LLC, an Internet-based media company that produced and distributed proprietary interactive celebrity based content. Counted among the most significant teen community web properties, Celebrity Sightings has been featured on Entertainment Tonight, Access Hollywood, CNN, E! Entertainment Television, and various other media outlets. In 1999 Celebrity Sightings was acquired by Alloy Online, a leading web site providing community, content, and commerce to Generation Y.

In 1998, Koch and partner, Len Grossi, started Mile Square Entertainment, Inc. Koch served as president and CO-CEO of the film and television development and production company. Mile Square Entertainment optioned and sold the feature film project "Murderer's Row" which is currently in development at Miramax. In addition, Koch created a new game show on behalf of Mile Square entitled "You Be the Judge" which was optioned by America's Funniest Videos creator, Vin DiBona.

Koch began his entertainment career as a partner in the Barbara Cameron Talent Agency. Now in its eleventh year, the agency is counted as one of the most powerful forces in the discovery and development of young talent. Koch's partner in the agency, Barbara Cameron, is the mother of Kirk Cameron ("Growing Pains") and Candace Cameron ("Full House").

Koch has, for the past four years, accepted the role as the pitch expert/instructor for the NATPE organization. The "How to Pitch Your Pitch" seminar has ranked at the top of attended seminars every year. Koch averages approximately ten speaking engagement per year.

In recognition of the contributions made by Gravy Train Productions, Koch was elected to the board of the Starlight Foundation, an organization that grants wishes to terminally ill children. Additionally, Koch has worked closely with the Pennsylvania State University based "Second Mile Program" which provides counseling and educational opportunities to underprivileged youth.

Robert Kosberg, "King of the Pitch," has been a producer on such projects as *Commando* (starring Arnold Schwarzenegger—Fox Studios) and *Twelve Monkeys* (starring Brad Pitt and Bruce Willis—Universal Studios). He currently has over twenty-five feature films in active development at various studios;

among these are *Surrender Dorothy* (Drew Barrymore, attached—Warner Brothers), *The Hardy Men* (Ben Stiller, attached—Fox Studios), and *Wild Pitch* (Adam Sandler, attached—Revolution Studios). As for TV, Kosberg produced "Mr. Personality." He is currently based at Nash Entertainment, which is known as one of the most prolific production companies in reality TV.

Tanya Meurer Norman is a writer, researcher, script doctor, story consultant, and editor. Her current projects include *Bikini Wax Confessions from the Cattle Baron's Ball, Tadpoling in the Summer of Demi Moore,* and "Steal This Chicken." Known for her one-on-one "pitch-tweaking sessions," she lectures at universities on the art of the pitch and pitch strategies.

More great Quill Driver Books' titles on writing & publishing!

The American Directory of
Writer's Guidelines, 4th Edition

A Compilation of Information for Freelancers from More than 1,500 Magazine Editors and Book Publishers

—Compiled and Edited by Brigitte M. Phillips, Susan D. Klassen and Doris Hall

Perhaps the best-kept secret in the publishing industry is that many publishers—both periodical publishers and book publishers—make available writer's guidelines to assist would-be contributors. Written by the staff at each publishing house, these guidelines help writers target their submissions to the exact needs of the individual publisher. *The American Directory of Writer's Guidelines* is a compilation of the actual writer's guidelines for more than 1,500 publishers.

$29.95 (*$45.00 Canada*)
• ISBN 1-884956-40-8
(*Replaces 3rd Edition, ISBN 1-884956-19-X*)
• Indexed by topics

" *Unlike the entries in Writer's Market (Writer's Digest, annual), which edits the information supplied by publishers and prints it in a standard entry format, this new resource contains unedited self-descriptions of publications and publishing houses.* **"**
—Booklist

Damn!
Why Didn't I Write That?

Book-of-the-Month Club, Quality Paperback Book Club, and Writer's Digest Book Club Selection!

How Ordinary People are Raking in $100,000.00... Or More Writing Nonfiction Books & How You Can Too!

—by Marc McCutcheon

More nonfiction books are breaking the 100,000-copy sales barrier than ever before. Amateur writers, housewives, and even high school dropouts have cashed in with astonishingly simple best-sellers. This guide, by best-selling author Marc McCutcheon, shows the reader how to get in on the action.

$14.95 (*$22.50 Canada*)
• ISBN 1-884956-17-3

" *Comprehensive and engaging this book will save you time, energy, and frustration.* **"**
—Michael Larsen, literary agent, author

Available at better brick and mortar bookstores, online bookstores, at
QuillDriverBooks.com, or by calling toll-free 1-800-497-4909

More great Quill Driver Books' titles on writing & publishing!

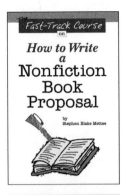

The Fast-Track Course
Nonfiction Book Proposal
—by Stephen Blake Mettee

Mettee, a seasoned book editor and publisher, cuts to the chase and provides simple, detailed instruction that allows anyone to write a professional book proposal and hear an editor say "Yes!"

$12.95 ($19.95 *Canada*)
• ISBN 1-884956-22-X

" *...essential, succinct guideline. This is a must have reference book for writers ...sets the industry standard.* **"**
—**Bob Spear,** *Heartland Reviews*

"*Every writer needs a book like this. Mettee's sound, practical advice is just the ticket to make an editor welcome a writer's work! Keep the book close by, because you'll use it—guaranteed!***"**
—**William Noble, author of** *Writing Dramatic Nonfiction*

Both titles are Writer's Digest Book Club Selections!

Quit Your Day Job!
How to Sleep Late, Do What You Enjoy, and Make a Ton of Money *as a Writer!*
—by Jim Denney

Resolution and perseverance are required to build a writing career and if you're going to succeed, you don't need the hype or hyperbole so often dished out in other writer's guides. You need a candid, no-nonsense appraisal of the daily grind of the writer's life, with the potholes and pitfalls clearly marked.

This book is your road map, written by someone who's lived the writing life for years, with more than sixty published novels and nonfiction books to his credit.

$14.95 (29.95 *Canada*)
• ISBN 1-884956-04-1

" *While there are always a few charmed souls, most career-bent writers are destined to struggle. Jim Denney has been there, done that. Read his book and save yourself much of the anguish.* **"**
—James N. Frey, author of *How to Write a Damn Good Novel*

Available at better brick and mortar bookstores, online bookstores, at
QuillDriverBooks.com, or by calling toll-free 1-800-497-4909

Still more great Quill Driver Books' titles on writing & publishing!

A Writer's Digest Book Club Selection!

The ABCs of
Writing for Children
**114 Children's Authors and Illustrators
Talk About the Art, the Business, the Craft
& the Life of Writing Children's Literature**
—*by Elizabeth Koehler-Pentacoff*

In *The ABCs of Writing for Children* you'll learn the many 'do's and don'ts' for creating children's books. You'll see that what works for one author may not work for the next.

❝ *...a thorough, complete, entertaining guide to writing for children—more alpha to omega than ABCs. I wish there was such a volume for every aspect of my life!* ❞
—**Karen Cushman, author of Catherine, Called Birdy**

$16.95 ($22.95 *Canada*)
• ISBN 1-884956-28-9

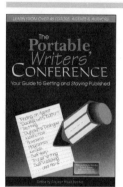

The Portable Writers' Conference
Your Guide to Getting and *Staying* Published
—*Edited by Stephen Blake Mettee*

Over 45 editors, authors, and agents advise writers on the art and business of writing and getting published. Chapters range from how to write a dynamite love scene to how to find an agent.

❝ *Here is the perfect way to attend a writers' conference...* ❞
—**Library Journal**

$19.95 ($29.95 *Canada*) • ISBN 1-884956-23-8

Both titles are Writer's Digest Book Club Selections!

Feminine Wiles
**Creative Techniques for Writing
Women's Feature Stories That *Sell***
—*by Donna Elizabeth Boetig*

From *Feminine Wiles*: ...commit yourself. You are going to write stories of women's struggles and joys. You are going to discover information that changes the lives of readers. You are going to predict trends and you may even create a few of your own. You are going to look out into the world to see what's happening and take what you find deep within yourself to figure out what it all means—for you, and your readers.

❝*More valuable than a dozen writer's workshops or journalism courses. If you're interested in developing a successful career as a freelance writer for women's magazines, read Feminine Wiles—and get to work.*❞
— **Jane Farrell, Senior Editor McCall's**

$14.95 ($21.95 *Canada*)
• ISBN 1-884956-02-5